WORDS WE ONCE KNEW

RECOVERING THE LANGUAGE THAT MAKES US HUMAN

JEFF GATLIN

LAURELWOOD PRESS

For my mother, who always said I should write a book.

And for Mary, who puts up with a lot of my words.

Contents

INTRODUCTION

The book that changed everything for me was purchased on a whim from Amazon. A thin paperback (about the size of the book in your hand right now) with a plain cover: *History in English Words* by Owen Barfield. I'd stumbled onto Barfield the way most people do—sideways. Reading one book often leads me to buy several more books, and discovering Barfield followed that progression. I'd been reading Tolkien since childhood, then moved to reading *about* Tolkien, which led me to the Inklings, which then led me to Tolkien's and Lewis's lesser-known friends, which eventually landed me here, holding this odd little book by a man who'd been a solicitor and a philosopher and something called an "Anthroposophist," whatever that was.

I started it tentatively, slowly, unsure at first what to make of both book and author. Then as I picked it up again on an autumn afternoon when I was supposed to be doing physical therapy exercises after a recent surgery, the message got through.

This little book hit differently.

Barfield's premise was simple: the history of a people lives inside their language. Not just *recorded* in language, but *preserved* in it—like fossils in rock, like rings in a tree. Every word we speak carries layers of meaning deposited by previous generations. When we say "nice," we're using a word that once meant "foolish," then "precise," then "pleasant." When we say "artificial," we're carrying a word that used to mean "full of art"—something worthy of admiration, not suspicion. The entire moral and intellectual history of English-speaking peoples, Barfield argued, could be traced through the words we've inherited and how their meanings have shifted, deepened, or thinned over time.

What struck me that October afternoon wasn't Barfield's method. It was his assumptions.

He assumed his readers still possessed a vocabulary with some thickness to it. He assumed they knew the difference between "sentiment" and "sentimentality," between "freedom" and "license," between "tolerance" and "indifference." He assumed they had encountered words like *reverence, gravity, duty*, and *honor* often enough to recognize what they meant—not just definitionally, but experientially. He wrote as though language still had depth, with regret that people do not use the full register of English, but rather the thin, exhausted slice we've grown accustomed to.

I realized, with something close to grief, that he was a "prophet crying in the wilderness." The English-speaking world wasn't getting better as Barfield wished, but worse. Language was getting thicker, but our vocabularies – like our consciousness – were thinning.

Something had happened to our language in the decades since Barfield wrote. Not a sudden collapse—nothing dramatic enough to name or date—but a gradual thinning. A leaching away of meaning. A loss of precision that had left us with words we could still technically use, but which no longer carried the weight they once did.

And it wasn't just the fancy words—the elevated, literary ones you'd expect to fall out of circulation. It was ordinary words. Essential words. *Common sense. Responsibility. Gratitude. Truth.* We still said them, but we said them differently. Lighter. Vaguer. With a kind of embarrassed distance, as if we weren't quite sure we believed in them anymore. Even worse, on a really bad day, we weaponized them.

I started paying attention.

I'm an engineer by education and profession, which means I've spent most of my working life in environments where language – including mathematics, which Galileo said was the language in which God wrote the universe—must be precise. When you're designing complex heating and cooling systems for critical environments or managing those that serve healthcare campuses, or calculating infrastructure capacities, you can't afford vagueness. "Pressure" is not the same as a "temperature", but yet they do have fixed relationships that must be respected. A "tolerance" is a measurable range, not a moral posture. Words in that world still mean what they mean, because the consequences of imprecision are sometimes immediate and often catastrophic.

But outside the technical world—in everyday conversation, in public discourse, in the cultural air we all breathe—I began noticing a different kind of imprecision. Not the innocent kind that comes from not knowing better, but the deliberate kind. Words were being used not to clarify but to obscure. Not to reveal but to manipulate. Not to connect but to shut down conversation.

Tolerance no longer meant the strength to endure disagreement; it meant the demand that others never cause you discomfort. *Safety* no longer referred to protection from physical harm; it described freedom from ideas that challenged you. *Hero* no longer implied sacrifice; it applied to anyone momentarily in the public eye. *Bigot* no longer named a specific moral failing; it had become a cudgel to silence dissent.

Even words I'd always thought of as stable—words like *gratitude, responsibility,* and *truth* — had begun to shift. Gratitude felt optional, something you performed when convenient. Responsibility sounded like a burden people tried to avoid rather than a dignity people chose to carry. And truth—well, truth had splintered into "my truth" and "your truth," as though reality itself were a matter of personal preference.

I watched friendships strain under the weight of this linguistic confusion. I watched workplaces fracture because people could no longer agree on what words meant. I watched families grow distant because conversations that used to unfold naturally now felt like navigating a minefield. Everywhere I looked, I saw people struggling to express things they still felt deeply but could no longer articulate with confidence and without fear.

Something had broken. And the break was in the language itself.

If Barfield were writing today, he'd have a lot to cover.

He'd need a chapter on how *common sense* — once the ballast of ordinary life—became something people apologized for invoking, as though it were embarrassingly unsophisticated. He'd need to trace how *safety* expanded from meaning "protection from danger" to meaning "protection from discomfort," and what that shift cost us in terms of resilience and intellectual courage. He'd have to explain how *hero* inflated to the point of meaninglessness, how *tolerance* inverted into intolerance, how *offense* stopped being something we interpreted and became something we weaponized.

He'd need to document the hollowing out of our moral vocabulary—the words we once used to describe the interior life and the life we share with others. Words like *reverence, duty, honor, dignity, humility*. Not because these realities have vanished, but because we've lost the language to name them clearly. And when you lose the language, you eventually lose the ability to recognize the thing itself.

This isn't a book about grammar or usage. It's not a plea to speak more formally or return to some imagined golden age of eloquence. It's an attempt to trace what Barfield traced—the history of a people through their words—but to do it for our moment, in our vernacular, with our particular confusions and losses in view.

I want to show how specific words thinned, and what that thinning has cost us. I want to recover some of the meanings we've forgotten or abandoned. And I want to suggest—carefully, without nostalgia—that we might still reclaim enough precision and depth in our language to make shared life possible again.

Because here's what I've learned since opening up Barfield that autumn afternoon: The thinning of language is not neutral. It changes us. When our words lose weight, so do our thoughts. When our vocabulary shrinks, so does our imagination. When reverence fades from our speech, it fades from our lives. Language is not merely a tool we use; it is the medium in which our interior lives take shape.

The structure of this book follows the order I needed myself. The first several chapters look at individual words and trace their decline—how they thinned, when, and why it matters. Each chapter focuses on a single word or cluster of words: *common sense, tolerance, safety, hero, bigot, gratitude, responsibility, truth, reverence.* I try to show what each word used to mean, what it means now, and what we've lost in the transition.

The middle chapters turn more personal—exploring how language shapes the actual texture of our lives. How it forms habits of love and listening. How it determines whether our homes feel safe or combative. How we either become the people our words assume we are, or we live divided against ourselves.

The final chapter is about stewardship—the quiet, unglamorous work of tending language so that the next generation inherits something they can actually use. It's about the small fidelities that restore meaning: speaking with intention, listening with patience, choosing clarity over performance, sincerity over spectacle.

I should say plainly that I haven't written this as someone who always gets language right. I've been shaped—often for better, sometimes for worse—by the same cultural forces I'm describing here. Whatever insight exists in these pages comes not from mastery, but from paying attention. From noticing how words work on us, and how we work on them.

The most prolific user of words I knew, who modeled reading and working crossword puzzles in front of me for most of my first sixty years, by example, indirectly taught me to love words is no longer able to use them. My mother spent decades as a kindergarten and children's Sunday school teacher. She filled rooms with stories, memories, observations, and a kind of warm, relentless narration of daily life. She never had a thought, my father used to tease, that didn't come out of her mouth. She loved the spoken language the way some people love music—instinctively, unselfconsciously, completely.

Then aphasia came. Sudden and thorough. The words she'd used her whole life began drifting beyond her reach. Sentences frayed. Meanings loosened. The woman who had narrated "every thought that went into her head" eventually fell nearly silent, not because she had nothing to say, but because the medium through which she'd always spoken had been taken from her.

Watching that happen taught me something no theory could: When we lose our words, we lose more than vocabulary. We lose the structures that hold our memories, the tools that shape our relationships, and the bridges that connect our inner world to the outer one. Language is not decoration. It is identity. It is meaning. It is part of what makes us capable of connection, memory, and hope.

Her story bookends this project. I arrived at the "why" of this book as I was struggling to wrap up the "how" and "how much". I have realized that it's why I care about vocabulary, why I pay attention to how words thin, and why I believe recovering depth in our language is not an academic exercise but a deeply human one.

So, this is an attempt to do what Barfield did—to trace the history of a people through their words—but for a moment when that history is harder to read because the words themselves have become unstable. It's a book about loss, yes, but also about recovery. About what happens when we stop taking language for granted and start treating it as something fragile, powerful, and worth preserving.

If these pages help you recover a word you'd forgotten, or see more clearly how language shapes your life, or give you the courage to speak with a little more care—then they'll have done what I hoped they'd do.

Because in the end, we don't just *use* language.

We become it.

ONE

COMMON SENSE

The world is full of obvious things which nobody by any chance ever observes.
—Arthur Conan Doyle, *The Hound of the Baskervilles*

There's a moment in every kind of work when someone has to say the obvious thing. There's a moment in Kipling's *The White Seal* that has always stayed with me. You don't have to remember the whole tale—just the broad strokes. Every year the seals return to the same beach out of habit, even though hunters come to that beach every year for the same reason. Everyone knows the danger. Everyone sees the blood in the surf. And yet they keep returning, simply because that's where they have always gone. And every year, hundreds of seals died. The elders always shrugged and said, *"This is the price of living. There is nowhere else."*

That's what happened to common sense.

Not all at once. Not through any single decision or event. It eroded the way coastlines do—grain by grain, so gradually that most people didn't notice until the shape of the land had changed completely. One day we woke up in a world where the obvious had become obscure, where basic patterns of cause and effect seemed debatable, where people could look directly at reality and somehow miss it entirely. Like the seals, we couldn't equate the bloody surf with the hunter's club.

Common sense used to mean something specific. It was the accumulation of practical knowledge gathered by paying attention to the world as it actually is, not as we wished it to be or feared it might become. It was the ability to distinguish real danger from imagined danger, real solutions from feel-good gestures, real patterns from coincidences. It wasn't brilliance. It wasn't expertise. It wasn't a specialized credential hanging on the office wall. It was the ballast of ordinary life—the shared foundation of assumptions so basic that people hardly needed to speak them aloud.

Fire burns. Gravity wins. People respond to incentives. Children need boundaries. Actions have consequences. A life without responsibility becomes unlivable. You can't borrow your way out of debt. If something sounds too good to be true, it probably is.

These weren't interesting observations. They were simply known—the way you know that winter follows fall, that rivers flow downhill, that a house built on sand won't stand as long as one built on rock. Common sense was the quiet agreement beneath all the noise, the baseline reality that allowed people to argue about details without losing sight of the essential.

And then we lost it.

The loss didn't look like stupidity. We didn't become less intelligent. We became less attentive.

Walk into any room today and you'll find people with access to more information than any generation in history. They can look up almost anything within seconds. They can fact-check claims in real time. They have immediate access in the palm of their hand to more data, more statistics, more studies, and more expert opinions than their grandparents could have imagined. But somewhere between the explosion of information and the collapse of attention, we stopped being able to see.

Not see as in "perceive with the eyes." See as in "recognize patterns." See as in "distinguish signal from noise." See as in "notice when something doesn't add up."

I started noticing this everywhere. In workplaces where people could recite company policy verbatim but couldn't figure out why morale kept tanking. In schools where administrators implemented elaborate anti-bullying programs while ignoring the fact that the kids eating lunch alone weren't being bullied—they were being ignored, which is worse. In churches where leaders fretted

Partly through abstraction. Common sense works best with concrete things. You can observe a child, a garden, a budget, a relationship, and learn their patterns. But when everything becomes theoretical—when we spend more time arguing about ideas than dealing with actual people, actual problems, actual constraints—common sense atrophies. It needs ground to stand on.

Partly through the collapse of shared experience. Common sense used to be transmitted through elders—people who'd lived through enough seasons to understand cycles, enough failures to recognize warning signs, enough hardship to separate the essential from the trivial. But we stopped listening to them. We decided their experience was obsolete, that everything had changed so much their wisdom no longer applied. So each generation now has to relearn lessons the hard way that could have been taught gently.

Partly through speed. Common sense develops slowly, through observation and repetition. And partly through shame. We made common sense embarrassing. If you invoked it, you were unsophisticated, uneducated, out of touch. The smart people dealt in theory, in data, in credentials. Common sense was for rubes. So people stopped trusting their own perceptions. They stopped saying, "Wait, this doesn't make sense," because they didn't want to look stupid. Better to nod along with the absurdity than risk being thought simple.

How, then, do we get it back?

It doesn't require new theories or elaborate programs. It asks only that we pay attention again—that we relearn the art of noticing, that we test our assumptions against the real world, that we allow feedback to correct us, that we give ourselves time to absorb experience rather than instantly react to it.

Most of the recovery happens in small, unseen ways. In the pause before responding to an email. In the moment you think before sharing an outrage on social media. In the quiet work of teaching a child to distinguish discomfort from actual danger. In refusing to outsource your judgment to crowds, algorithms, or experts who don't know your life. In accepting that reality has structure, that some truths are indifferent to your preferences, and that consequences eventually arrive whether you believe in them or not.

Common sense returns when someone finally says, "The emperor has no clothes," and others realize they'd been thinking the same thing but were afraid to speak. It returns when people stop pretending that obvious problems aren't problems. It returns when communities decide that noticing reality is more important than maintaining comfortable fictions.

It won't happen dramatically. It will happen the way erosion happens—slowly, in a thousand small choices, in the daily decision to trust what you can see over what you're told you should see.

Kotick, Kipling's white seal, understood this instinctively. Not because he was smarter than the other seals, but because he refused to accept that bloody surf was just *'the price of living.'* He trusted what he could see.

That's common sense. Not a theory. Not a credential. Just the practiced habit of seeing what's actually there.

And recovering it begins the moment you decide the obvious is worth noticing again.

The erosion of common sense has been so gradual that most people haven't noticed it happening. It didn't announce itself. There was no single moment when society decided to stop trusting observable reality in favor of abstract theory. Instead, it happened through a thousand small accommodations, each one seeming reasonable in isolation, each one making the next accommodation easier.

First, we accepted that expertise should always trump experience. If the studies said one thing and your lying eyes said another, you learned to distrust your eyes. This seemed wise—after all, systematic study should reveal truths that casual observation might miss. But it created a dependency: people stopped trusting their own judgment and started waiting for experts to tell them what to think.

Then we accepted that feelings could be evidence. If someone felt harmed, harm must have occurred. If someone felt unsafe, danger must be present. This seemed compassionate—after all, people's experiences matter. But it severed the connection between subjective experience and objective reality. It made verification impossible. How do you test whether someone really feels unsafe? You can't.

So you have to accept the claim at face value, which means you've abandoned common sense.

Finally, we accepted that disagreement itself might be harmful. Not disagreement expressed cruelly—just disagreement. The existence of contrary opinions became something people needed protection from. This seemed kind—after all, why subject people to ideas that distress them? But it made rational discourse impossible. Because rational discourse requires the ability to encounter ideas you find wrong, objectionable, even abhorrent, and respond to them with argument rather than demands for protection.

Each of these moves seemed defensible. Each addressed a real concern. But together, they dismantled the infrastructure of common sense. They created a world where reality is whatever someone insists it is, where observable facts matter less than asserted feelings, where the obvious thing can't be said because saying it might cause distress.

The recovery of common sense doesn't require a dramatic revolution. It requires a modest return to something simple: the willingness to notice what's in front of you and say it out loud, even when saying it feels risky.

Two

TOLERANCE

"Be tolerant with others and strict with yourself."
—Marcus Aurelius

In 2018, a biology professor at a state university mentioned in class that biological sex exists as a category distinct from gender identity. She wasn't arguing against anyone's dignity. She wasn't denying anyone's experience. She was teaching basic biology—the kind that's been taught for decades without incident. Two students filed a complaint. Within a week, she was meeting with administrators who told her that several students now felt unsafe in her classroom. The word *unsafe* appeared repeatedly in the incident report. Not uncomfortable. Not challenged. Not disagreeing. Unsafe. The professor wasn't fired. She wasn't formally disciplined. But the message was clear: some topics, even in a biology classroom, had become too dangerous to discuss. By the end of the semester, she'd begun avoiding entire areas of inquiry—not because they weren't scientifically relevant, but because she could no longer predict what might be called harmful.

This wasn't an isolated case. It has become a pattern. Search "professor disciplined" and you'll find dozens of similar stories from the last five years alone. Different campuses, different disciplines, different specific triggers—but the same basic script: someone states a view that was uncontroversial a decade ago, students claim harm, the institution responds by treating disagreement as a threat to safety.

Or consider what happened in a Colorado public library in 2019. A religious group reserved a meeting room—the same kind of room available to any community organization. They planned to discuss traditional Christian views on marriage. Before the meeting even occurred, other community members demanded the library cancel the reservation. Not because the group had broken any rules. Not because they'd been disruptive in the past. But because their views, simply by being expressed in a public building, would make others "feel unwelcome." The library initially defended the reservation—meeting rooms are public forums, open to all viewpoints. But the pressure mounted. Petitions circulated. The library received calls claiming that allowing the meeting was itself a form of discrimination. Eventually, the library canceled, citing "community standards" and "creating a welcoming environment." The message was unmistakable: tolerance now meant preventing certain people from speaking at all, even in spaces explicitly designed for diverse community use. The meeting room sat empty that night—safe, welcoming, and perfectly sterile.

That's what happened to tolerance.

Tolerance used to be one of the modest but essential virtues of democratic life.

It didn't mean *agreement*. It didn't mean *approval*. It didn't even mean you had to like the person whose views you were tolerating. Tolerance was simply the strength to endure difference without collapsing into hostility. It was the recognition that in a free society, people would hold incompatible beliefs—sometimes deeply, sometimes passionately—and that the task of adulthood was to live with others alongside that tension without treating it as an emergency.

Marcus Aurelius understood this. "Be *tolerant with others and strict with yourself*." The formulation is elegant because it's asymmetrical. Tolerance wasn't about lowering standards. It was about directing your moral energy inward—holding yourself to account while extending patience outward. It assumed that your own character was the proper object of your scrutiny, not someone else's.

The older form of tolerance required something we are growing increasingly uncomfortable with: interior strength. You had to be stable enough within yourself to let other people be wrong. You had to possess enough confidence in your own convictions that you didn't need everyone around you to validate them constantly. Tolerance was what you practiced when you were secure.

It also assumed something else we have largely forgotten: *that disagreement was normal.* Not pathological. Not a sign that something had gone wrong. Just the natural state of human beings thinking for themselves. In a country of hundreds of millions of people with different backgrounds, experiences, and prior commitments, of course there would be friction. Tolerance was the grease that kept the friction from becoming fire.

But tolerance in that older sense asked something of the people practicing it. It asked them to develop a thicker skin, to distinguish between harm and discomfort, to resist the impulse to treat every challenge as an assault. It put the burden on the individual to grow strong enough to endure difference.

Modern tolerance has inverted the burden entirely.

Somewhere along the way—gradually, perhaps imperceptibly at first—tolerance stopped being something you practiced and became something you demanded. The expectation shifted from "I will tolerate you" to "You must not disturb me!" Instead of developing resilience, we began designing environments to eliminate anything that might require it.

The language changed accordingly. We stopped saying "I disagree" and started saying "That's harmful." We stopped saying "I'm offended" and started saying "I'm unsafe" or "You are offensive." We stopped distinguishing between speech that threatens and speech that challenges. And once that distinction collapsed, tolerance became impossible—because if disagreement itself is harm, then tolerance isn't a virtue. It's complicity.

This shift shows up everywhere, but it's most visible in institutions that once prided themselves on intellectual diversity.

Universities invented the "safe space"—not as a temporary refuge for someone processing trauma, but as a permanent posture toward the world. The idea was reasonable enough at first: create environments where students could speak openly without fear of social punishment. But it metastasized. Soon, safety wasn't about protection from cruelty; it was about protection from discomfort. And since discomfort is inevitable wherever people think seriously about complicated things, the only way to maintain safety was to stop thinking seriously about complicated things.

Workplaces followed. Diversity and inclusion training—intended to help people work together across differences—became exercises in linguistic tripwire identification. Employees learned which words were forbidden, which questions were dangerous, which opinions marked you as backward. The goal shifted from "How do we work together despite our differences?" to "How do we eliminate difference?"

Even families and friendships fragmented along these lines. People stopped talking about politics, religion, or morality—not because these things didn't matter, but because no one trusted that even a minor disagreement could be survived. Thanksgiving dinners became minefields. Old friendships quietly ended not because of any specific betrayal, but because someone liked the wrong post, called her friend the wrong pronoun, or failed to express the right degree of enthusiasm for the right cause. Tolerance wasn't needed because association itself had become conditional on agreement.

The cruel irony is that this supposedly tolerant approach has made us less capable of living together.

Here's what the new tolerance looks like in practice.

In 2016, dozens of schools across the country began removing *To Kill a Mockingbird* from their curricula. The novel—taught for decades as a text about racism, injustice, and moral courage—came under fire not for its themes but for its language. It uses a racial slur, historically accurate to the setting, spoken by characters the novel itself condemns. Parents and students said it made them uncomfortable. Schools, rather than distinguish between depicting racism and endorsing it, pulled the book.

What gets lost isn't just a novel. It's the ability to encounter difficult things in a mediated, thoughtful environment—which is exactly what education is supposed to provide. But tolerance in its new form can't allow difficulty. It can't let students sit with discomfort long enough to think through it. It must protect them from the encounter itself. Fortunately, for both language and society, the quickest way to renew interest in a book, or any artistic work, is for the establishment to ban it.

Or consider what happens in the average workplace meeting when someone proposes a new policy. A colleague raises a practical concern—not a hostile objection, just a question about implementation. Immediately, someone else interjects: "I don't think that question is helpful." Not incorrect. Not based on a misunderstanding. Just "not helpful". The subtext is clear: your question creates discomfort, and discomfort is now treated as a form of aggression. The meeting continues, but the policy isn't improved, because the mechanism for improving it—honest questioning—has been shut down in the name of tolerance.

Or take what's become a familiar pattern at family gatherings: someone's uncle makes an offhand comment—clumsy, maybe, but not malicious. Instead of someone gently correcting him or letting it pass, the room goes silent. Later, someone posts about it on social media. The uncle becomes a symbol of everything wrong with "that generation." He's not educated; he's erased. He's not engaged; he's dismissed. And the family fractures a little more because tolerance no longer means enduring the uncle. It means expelling him.

In each case, the mechanism is the same: instead of developing the strength to endure disagreement, we eliminate the disagreement. Instead of growing thicker skin, we demand thinner speech. Instead of learning to live with tension, we exile anyone who creates it.

And then we call this tolerance.

The most insidious thing about the new tolerance is that it feels virtuous. It feels like compassion. It feels like protecting the vulnerable. It feels like standing up for people who've been hurt. And sometimes—sometimes—it actually is those things. There are moments when speech genuinely harms, when environments genuinely threaten, when the right response is intervention.

But we've lost the ability to distinguish those moments from ordinary disagreement.

A student who says "I feel unsafe because someone used a slur against me" is describing a real problem that requires a real response. A student who says "I feel unsafe because someone argued that sex and gender are distinct categories" is describing discomfort, not danger. The two are not equivalent. But if we treat them as equivalent—if every claim of harm is taken at face value without scrutiny—then tolerance becomes impossible, because everything can be framed as harm.

And here's what makes it especially difficult: the people demanding this new form of tolerance genuinely believe they're fighting intolerance. They see themselves as protecting the marginalized, challenging the powerful, creating a more just world. And in some cases, they are. But in many cases, they're simply enforcing conformity—and conformity, however well-intentioned, is the opposite of tolerance.

True tolerance doesn't mean endorsing everything. It doesn't mean pretending every view is equally valid. It means allowing people to be wrong without destroying them for it. It means making space for disagreement, even heated disagreement, without treating disagreement itself as violence. It means accepting that in a pluralistic society, people will hold views you find foolish, offensive, or even abhorrent—and that the cost of freedom is letting them hold those views anyway.

Marcus Aurelius had it right. The tolerance that matters is the tolerance you practice when you're frustrated, when someone's views genuinely bother you, when you'd much rather they just shut up and conform. That's when tolerance does its real work. That's when it protects something larger than your momentary comfort.

The tragedy is that we once knew how to do this.

For most of American history, people managed to live alongside deep disagreements without demanding that one side surrender or disappear. Catholics and Protestants, who'd spent centuries killing each other in Europe, learned to be neighbors. Immigrants from dozens of countries, speaking different languages and practicing different customs, somehow formed communities. People with wildly different views on religion, politics, economics, and morality shared towns, workplaces, and sometimes even dinner tables.

It wasn't always peaceful. There were failures—catastrophic ones. But the default assumption was that difference was permanent and tolerance was necessary. You didn't have to like your neighbor's views. You just had to let them hold those views without treating their existence as a threat to yours.

That assumption has eroded. We've replaced it with something newer, something that sounds more sophisticated but functions far more rigidly: the idea that tolerance means creating spaces where no one ever has to encounter a view that challenges them. Where safety means protection not from violence but from disagreement. Where inclusion means uniformity of thought.

This isn't progress. It is regression disguised as enlightenment. Because a society that can't tolerate disagreement can't tolerate freedom. And a society that can't tolerate freedom eventually can't tolerate much of anything—including the people who once believed they were building something better.

So how do we recover tolerance?

Not the new version, which isn't tolerance at all, but the old version—the sturdy, modest virtue that lets people with incompatible beliefs live, work, and exist in the same society without demanding that one side vanish.

First, we have to recover the distinction between harm and discomfort.

Not everything that makes you uncomfortable is harming you. This seems obvious when stated plainly, but we've spent the last decade systematically erasing this distinction until the two have become functionally interchangeable. A student who hears an argument she disagrees with reports feeling "harmed." An employee who's asked to consider a perspective different from his own describes the experience as "traumatic." A reader who encounters an opinion piece with an opposing viewpoint says the publication has "platforming violence." The language has become so inflated that we've lost the ability to calibrate our responses to actual threats.

Real harm has specific characteristics. It involves direct action against someone's body, property, or rights. It creates tangible damage that can be identified and measured. A person who's physically assaulted has been harmed. A person who's been fired for their race has been harmed. A person who's been denied housing because of their religion has been harmed. These are genuine violations that require genuine responses—legal, institutional, social. Discomfort is different.

Discomfort is what you feel when your assumptions are questioned, when someone presents evidence that contradicts your beliefs, when you encounter a worldview that makes your own seem less certain. Discomfort is what happens when you're forced to think rather than simply react. It's uncomfortable precisely because it's doing something—not to you, but in you. It's the friction of growth.

Much of education, in fact, should make you uncomfortable. A literature class that never assigns books with disturbing themes isn't teaching literature—it's teaching avoidance. A history class that never discusses the genuine moral failures of the past isn't teaching history—it's teaching mythology. A science class that never presents theories that challenge students' prior beliefs isn't teaching science—it's teaching catechism. Growth happens at the edge of comfort, not in its center. Learning requires exposure to ideas that disturb your equilibrium. If we can't distinguish discomfort from danger, we can't distinguish education from assault.

Consider what this looks like in practice. A college freshman takes a philosophy course and encounters an argument for moral relativism that conflicts with everything she was raised to believe. She finds it deeply unsettling. She goes to office hours and tells her professor, "That reading made me uncomfortable." The professor has two options. Option one: validate her discomfort as harm, apologize for assigning disturbing material, and perhaps offer an alternative reading that won't challenge her beliefs. Option two: acknowledge her discomfort as evidence that she's engaging seriously with difficult ideas, and help her work through the argument on its merits. The first option protects her from discomfort. The second option teaches her to think. Only the second option is actually education.

The same principle applies outside the classroom. A coworker makes an argument you find offensive. You have two options: claim harm and demand he be silenced, or recognize your discomfort as disagreement and engage with his actual reasoning. A family member holds a political view you consider backwards.

You can treat her presence at Thanksgiving as a threat to your safety, or you can recognize that tolerating her presence—and even her wrongness—is what family and citizenship require. The ability to distinguish harm from discomfort is what makes tolerance possible. Without it, every encounter with difference becomes an emergency.

This doesn't mean all discomfort is good or that we should deliberately seek to offend. It means that discomfort alone isn't sufficient justification for demanding someone stop speaking. If we can't hear things that make us uncomfortable, we can't hear anything that might change our minds—which means we can't learn, and we certainly can't live with people who see the world differently.

Second, we have to recover the expectation of resilience.

A free society depends on citizens who are strong enough to hear things they don't like without demanding institutional intervention every time their feelings are hurt. This isn't cruelty. It's basic citizenship. In a country of 330 million people with wildly different backgrounds, experiences, and convictions, you are going to encounter views you find foolish, offensive, or even abhorrent on a regular basis. If your response to every such encounter is to appeal to an authority figure to make the bad man stop talking, you're not practicing citizenship—you're practicing childhood.

Resilience doesn't mean callousness. It doesn't mean pretending words don't affect you or that emotional responses are weakness. It means having the internal strength to encounter opposition without shattering. It means being secure enough in your own convictions that someone else's disagreement doesn't constitute a crisis. It means possessing the emotional stability to hear an argument you despise and respond with a counterargument rather than a demand for silence.

We used to understand this as a basic requirement of adulthood. Children needed protection from certain kinds of speech because they lacked the cognitive and emotional tools to process difficult ideas. Adults were expected to have developed those tools. The whole point of maturation was building the internal resources to handle conflict, disagreement, and discomfort without external intervention. We called this growing up.

Somewhere along the way, we decided this expectation was oppressive. We began treating emotional fragility not as a problem to overcome but as a status to be honored. We invented concepts like "emotional labor" to describe the ordinary work of managing your own reactions to the world. We created "self-care" routines that treated everyday interactions as traumatic events requiring recovery periods. We built entire institutional structures around the premise that people shouldn't have to develop resilience because the world should simply become less challenging.

The result is a generation of adults who've never developed the psychological immune system necessary for democratic life. They've been protected from discomfort so consistently that they experience ordinary disagreement as assault. They've been taught that their emotional reactions are always valid and never to be questioned, which means they've never learned to interrogate whether their feelings are proportional to the situation. They've been told that demanding others adjust to accommodate their sensitivities is a form of justice rather than a failure of self-governance.

This isn't compassion. It's cruelty disguised as care. Because the world doesn't care about your feelings, and no amount of institutional protection will change that. The person who's never developed resilience isn't being protected—they're being disabled. They're being rendered incapable of functioning in any environment that hasn't been specifically engineered for their comfort. And since most of life happens in environments that haven't been engineered for anyone's comfort, this is a recipe for perpetual suffering.

Consider what happens to someone who's been raised in an environment of maximum protection. She goes to college and encounters a professor who challenges her beliefs. Instead of engaging with the challenge, she files a complaint. The complaint succeeds—the professor is disciplined, the syllabus is revised, the uncomfortable reading is removed. She graduates and enters a workplace. A coworker makes a comment she finds offensive. She reports it to HR. HR intervenes. The coworker is sent to sensitivity training. The comment isn't repeated. She's learned a powerful lesson: the world will adjust to protect her from discomfort.

But then she encounters a situation where that pattern breaks down. Maybe she changes jobs and the new workplace doesn't have the same protections. Maybe she enters a relationship with someone who won't walk on eggshells. Maybe she simply encounters an aspect of life—illness, loss, failure—that can't be managed by appealing to an authority figure. And she has no tools to handle it because she's never had to develop any. Her entire strategy for dealing with difficulty has been to make someone else eliminate the difficulty. When that stops working, she's helpless.

That's not resilience. That's learned helplessness dressed up as empowerment. And it's what we're systematically teaching people by refusing to expect strength from them.

Recovering resilience means recovering the expectation that adults should be able to handle disagreement without intervention. It means praising strength rather than fragility. It means recognizing that the goal isn't to eliminate all discomfort from life—it's to build people capable of enduring discomfort without collapsing. It means understanding that you do someone no favors by protecting them from every challenge. You only prepare them for failure.

Third, we have to practice disagreement.

Actual disagreement, not the performative kind that happens on social media. The kind that happens face-to-face, where you have to see the other person as a full human being, not a caricature. The kind where you might not change their mind, but you don't storm out either. The kind that strengthens relationship rather than ending it.

We've lost this skill almost entirely. Most people now have so little experience with genuine disagreement that they've come to see it as inherently hostile. They confuse disagreement with disrespect, argument with attack, challenge with contempt. They've learned to interpret any questioning of their views as a personal assault, which means they've never learned how to separate their ideas from their identity. If you are your opinions, then any challenge to your opinions becomes a challenge to your existence. And if disagreement is existential threat, then tolerance becomes impossible.

But disagreement used to be understood as something different—not as a threat to relationship but as a form of relationship. Two people who disagreed sharply on important questions could still be friends, colleagues, even family, because they understood that disagreement didn't require enmity. You could think someone was completely wrong about politics, religion, or morality and still respect their character, trust their intentions, and value their presence in your life. The disagreement was real, but it wasn't total. You were more than your opinions, and so were they.

This required certain skills that we've largely stopped teaching. You had to learn how to state your position clearly without caricaturing the opposing view. You had to learn how to listen to arguments you found absurd without assuming the person making them was stupid or evil. You had to learn how to identify genuine points of disagreement instead of arguing past each other. You had to learn how to recognize when you'd reached an impasse and how to step back from the argument without stepping back from the relationship. None of this was easy, but all of it was learnable—and necessary.

Consider what this looks like when it's done well. Two coworkers disagree about a significant policy question. One thinks the company should prioritize growth; the other thinks it should prioritize sustainability. They both have good reasons for their positions. They both care about the company's future. They make their arguments clearly. They listen to each other's reasoning. They identify where they actually disagree—not on values, but on predictions about what will happen under different scenarios. They recognize that neither of them can prove their case definitively. They make their recommendations to leadership and accept whatever decision gets made. Then they go to lunch.

This isn't a particularly dramatic example, but that's the point. This is what normal disagreement looks like when people know how to do it. No one claims harm. No one accuses the other of bad faith. No one demands that HR intervene to protect them from their colleague's differing opinion. They simply disagree, make their cases, and continue working together.

Now consider what the same scenario looks like when people don't know how to disagree. The first person makes their argument for prioritizing growth. The second person doesn't engage with the argument—instead, they say, "That perspective centers profit over people." The first person, now defensive, responds, "I guess some of us care about keeping the company solvent." The second person takes this as a personal attack: "I can't believe you just implied I don't care about the company's survival." Within minutes, what could have been a substantive policy debate has become a conflict about character and motive. Both people leave angry. One of them emails HR. The next meeting is tense. The disagreement never gets resolved because it never actually got discussed—it just metastasized into mutual resentment.

The difference between these scenarios isn't the disagreement itself—it's whether the people involved know how to have disagreements. And increasingly, they don't, because they've had so little practice. We've created environments—online and offline—where disagreement is treated as dangerous, where the easiest path is simply to avoid anyone who might challenge your views. The result is that when disagreement becomes unavoidable, people have no idea how to handle it except through conflict or retreat.

Practicing disagreement means deliberately engaging with people who see things differently. It means reading arguments you expect to disagree with, not to find flaws you can mock, but to understand why someone might find them convincing. It means having conversations about contentious topics without the goal being to win or to change the other person's mind—just to understand their reasoning and to clarify your own. It means staying in relationships with people whose politics you find misguided, whose religious views you don't share, whose life choices you wouldn't make. Not because you're indifferent to truth, but because you recognize that living with difference is part of what it means to live in a free society.

This takes courage. It's much easier to curate your world until everyone sounds like you, to dismiss dissenters as backwards or bigoted, to surround yourself with people who affirm everything you already believe. But that's not tolerance. That's tribalism. And tribalism, however comfortable it feels, eventually leads to the kind of society where people can't talk to each other at all—which means they can't live together either.

Fourth, we have to relearn humility.

Real tolerance comes from the recognition that you might be wrong. Not about everything—some truths are worth holding firmly—but about enough things that you extend patience to others who see differently. Certainty kills tolerance. Humility sustains it.

The person who's absolutely sure they're right about everything has no reason to tolerate anyone who disagrees. If you possess perfect knowledge of morality, politics, and truth, then anyone who disagrees with you isn't just wrong—they're either stupid or wicked. And why would you tolerate stupidity or wickedness? The only logical response is to correct them if possible or exclude them if not. Absolute certainty leads inevitably to intolerance, because tolerance requires admitting at least the possibility that the other person might have something worth hearing.

Humility doesn't mean abandoning your convictions. It doesn't mean pretending all views are equally valid or that truth is just a matter of perspective. It means holding your convictions while acknowledging your limitations. It means recognizing that your understanding is partial, your information is incomplete, and your reasoning—however careful—might contain errors you haven't detected yet. It means accepting that even on questions where you're very confident, there might be considerations you haven't fully grasped.

This is harder than it sounds, especially in a culture that treats certainty as strength and doubt as weakness. We've been taught to present our views with maximum confidence, to never admit uncertainty, to treat questions as attacks and revision as defeat. Politicians who change their minds are derided as flip-floppers. Scholars who acknowledge the limits of their knowledge are seen as weak.

Anyone who says "I'm not sure" or "I might be wrong about this" is treated as if they've forfeited their right to be taken seriously.

But actually, it's the opposite. The person who admits uncertainty is demonstrating intellectual honesty. The person who changes their mind in response to evidence is showing integrity. The person who holds their convictions lightly enough to examine them is showing real confidence—the kind that doesn't need to pretend infallibility to maintain itself.

Consider what humility looks like in the context of tolerance. You hold a strong conviction about a political question—let's say immigration policy. You've thought about it carefully. You've read widely. You've considered counterarguments. You're genuinely confident your position is correct. But you also recognize that people who disagree with you aren't necessarily fools or monsters. They might have different values that lead to different conclusions. They might be weighing the same evidence differently. They might have experiences that shape their perspective in ways your experiences don't. You might be missing something important that they see clearly.

This recognition doesn't require you to abandon your position. You can still believe you're right and argue forcefully for your view. But it changes how you engage with disagreement. Instead of treating opposition as something to be crushed, you treat it as something to be understood. You make your case, but you also listen to theirs. You defend your reasoning, but you also examine it for weaknesses. You hold your ground, but you don't claim the ground is unassailable.

This is what Marcus Aurelius meant by *be tolerant with others and strict with yourself.* The strictness is directed inward—at your own reasoning, your own motives, your own certainty. The tolerance is directed outward—toward others who've reached different conclusions. It's the recognition that the proper object of your scrutiny is yourself, not other people.

Humility also requires recognizing how much of what you believe is contingent on factors outside your control. You were born in a particular place, to particular parents, in a particular era. You were shaped by experiences you didn't choose and influenced by people you didn't select. Much of what seems obviously true to you seems that way partly because of accidents of biography. Someone born in different circumstances, with equal intelligence and equal sincerity, might reach very different conclusions. This doesn't mean all conclusions are equally valid—some are still better reasoned than others. But it does mean you should hold your conclusions with enough humility to recognize that they're not purely the product of your superior reasoning. They're partly the product of your particular vantage point.

The alternative to humility is the kind of brittle certainty that makes tolerance impossible. It's the mindset that says, "I know I'm right, therefore anyone who disagrees is wrong, therefore I have no obligation to tolerate their wrongness." It's what happens when you confuse confidence with knowledge and conviction with truth. And it's what leads, inevitably, to the kind of society where disagreement becomes grounds for exclusion, where difference becomes threat, where tolerance dies because no one believes they need it anymore.

Recovering humility means recovering the capacity to say "I think I'm right, but I might be wrong" without feeling like you've undermined your own position. It means understanding that tolerance isn't weakness—it's the strength to live with uncertainty. It means recognizing that a free society depends not on everyone reaching the same conclusions, but on everyone being humble enough to let others reach different ones.

And finally, we have to remember that tolerance isn't about creating a world without conflict. It's about creating a world where conflict doesn't have to mean destruction. Where people can disagree sharply, even passionately, and still treat each other as neighbors. Where difference is seen not as a problem to be solved, but as a permanent feature of human life that requires ongoing, disciplined coexistence.

That's not easy. It's much easier to demand agreement, to exile dissenters, to curate your social world until everyone sounds like you. But ease is not the goal. Freedom is. And freedom cannot survive without tolerance—the real kind, the old kind, the kind that asks something difficult of us.

THREE

SAFETY

The truth does not change according to our ability to stomach it.
—Flannery O'Connor

Safety has suffered the same corruption as tolerance, but the trajectory runs even deeper into our psychology. Where tolerance governs how we respond to other people's beliefs, *safety* governs how we respond to reality itself. The pattern will sound familiar—a word that once meant something specific and measurable has expanded to include anything that makes us uncomfortable. But the stakes are different here. When tolerance fails, we lose the ability to live with people who think differently. When safety fails, we lose the ability to face the world as it actually is.

Both corruptions stem from the same cultural impulse: the belief that discomfort is harm, that challenge is threat, that the proper response to difficulty is elimination rather than navigation. But safety takes this impulse and applies it not to disagreement but to development itself—to the very process by which human beings grow capable of handling a world that doesn't care about their feelings.

The word *safety* used to mean something specific. It referred to protection from objective, measurable harm—the kind of danger that could injure the body, destroy property, or threaten life.

In 2019, a Massachusetts elementary school removed its playground equipment—swings, monkey bars, seesaws—after a series of minor injuries. No broken bones. No serious incidents. Just the ordinary scrapes and bruises that children have accumulated since playgrounds were invented. But the school board, concerned about liability and parental complaints, decided the risk was unacceptable. They installed rubber mats and low, rounded structures that made injuries from falling nearly impossible.

Within a year, teachers noticed something strange. The children had become more reckless, not less. Without the feedback of minor consequences—the sting of a scraped knee, the jolt of falling from a height that wasn't quite safe—they'd lost their ability to judge risk. They didn't learn caution; they learned fearlessness in the wrong contexts and timidity in safe ones. The playground had been made physically safer, but the children themselves had become less safe.

That's the paradox at the heart of modern safety culture: the more we protect people from encountering risk, the less capable they become of navigating it.

The word *safety* used to mean protection from real dangers that required real precautions. Safety meant building codes, seatbelts, handrails, fire exits. It meant systems designed to keep people alive and intact in a world that contained genuine threats.

Then, quietly and almost imperceptibly, the word expanded. It began to include emotional comfort, psychological ease, and freedom from disagreement. "I feel unsafe" gradually drifted from describing physical threat to describing discomfort, offense, or ideological tension. And once that shift occurred, safety became something else entirely—something subjective, unmeasurable, and ultimately impossible to achieve.

The original meaning of safety was objective because danger is objective.

A bridge either supports the weight placed on it or it collapses. A chemical either burns skin on contact or it doesn't. A live electrical wire either delivers a lethal shock or it's properly insulated. These aren't matters of opinion or feeling. They're matters of physics, chemistry, and biology. Safety measures exist because the world contains non-negotiable realities that will harm you regardless of whether you believe in them.

This is why safety culture in technical fields has always been rigorous. In engineering, manufacturing, aviation, medicine—anywhere consequences arrive swiftly and visibly—safety protocols are specific, measurable, and constantly tested against reality. You don't ask people how they feel about a load-bearing calculation. You test it. You verify it. You assume that if your math is wrong, the structure will fail, and people will get hurt.

The same principle applied to more everyday forms of safety. Parents taught children not to touch hot stoves, not because it might hurt their feelings, but because it would burn their hands. Schools enforced playground rules not to prevent hurt feelings but to prevent broken bones. Communities established traffic laws not to make people feel comfortable but to prevent collisions. The goal was always mitigation of real, physical harm.

But safety in that older sense asked something of people. It asked them to learn from consequences, to develop judgment, to understand cause and effect. A child who touched a hot stove once learned not to do it again—not through a lecture, but through direct feedback from reality. A teenager who drove too fast and got pulled over learned the relationship between speed and danger, or at least legal consequences. Safety wasn't about eliminating all risk; it was about teaching people to navigate risk intelligently.

This understanding began to erode in the 1990s and accelerated through the 2000s. The shift happened gradually, across multiple domains—parenting, education, workplace culture, public discourse—but the pattern was consistent: safety stopped being about protection from objective harm and became about protection from discomfort.

The expansion of "safety" into the emotional realm didn't happen through a single decision. It accumulated through a series of small, seemingly reasonable adjustments.

Universities led the way. In the early 2000s, many campuses created "safe spaces"—designated rooms where students dealing with trauma could find temporary refuge and support. The concept was modest and defensible: some students, especially survivors of assault or abuse, needed places where they could process difficult experiences without additional stress. The spaces were meant to be therapeutic, not permanent.

But the concept metastasized. "Safe space" expanded from a clinical intervention into a general philosophy. Soon it wasn't just about protecting trauma survivors; it was about protecting everyone from anything that might cause psychological distress. And since almost anything could theoretically cause distress—a challenging idea, an uncomfortable fact, a dissenting opinion—the definition of safety grew to encompass nearly everything.

By the 2010s, "I don't feel safe" had become a common phrase in classrooms, not in response to threats but in response to disagreement. A professor assigning a text with difficult content would hear students say they felt unsafe. A speaker invited to campus with controversial views would prompt claims of unsafety before they'd even arrived. The word had detached from its physical moorings entirely.

Children's lives were restructured around emotional safety. Schools eliminated competitive games to protect self-esteem. Parents began "bubble-wrapping" childhood—removing every sharp edge, every challenge, every moment where a child might fail or feel bad. Participation trophies replaced genuine achievement. Grade inflation became standard. The message to children was clear: *you should never have to feel uncomfortable, and if you do, adults will intervene to eliminate the source of discomfort.*

The result? A generation of young adults who struggle with basic resilience. College counseling centers report unprecedented demand for mental health services, not because students face greater objective dangers than previous generations, but because they've been trained to interpret ordinary stress as crisis. Anxiety and depression rates have skyrocketed, particularly among young people—despite living in the safest, wealthiest, most materially comfortable era in human history.

The paradox is stark: the more we protect people from discomfort, the more fragile they become.

Here's what the conflation of safety with comfort looks like in practice.

In 2017, students at several universities demanded that administrators cancel speeches by controversial public figures. Not because these speakers had threatened violence. Not because they'd advocated breaking laws. But because their ideas made students "feel unsafe." The rationale was straightforward: if hearing certain views causes psychological distress, and psychological distress is harm, then expressing those views is a form of violence. Therefore, preventing the speech is an act of protection.

The logic seems airtight—until you notice that it makes disagreement itself intolerable. If any idea that challenges your worldview can be labeled "unsafe," then no debate is possible. Universities, which have historically existed precisely to expose students to ideas they haven't encountered before, become places where only pre-approved thoughts are allowed. Safety becomes indistinguishable from censorship.

Or consider the now-common practice of trigger warnings. Originally intended to help trauma survivors prepare for content that might genuinely re-traumatize them—such as graphic depictions of sexual violence—trigger warnings expanded to cover virtually any topic someone might find upsetting. Professors were expected to warn students before discussing racism, war, colonialism, mental illness, or even unhappy endings in novels. The assumption was that exposure to difficult content was itself dangerous.

But education requires exposure to difficult content. History is full of atrocities. Literature explores tragedy. Philosophy raises unsettling questions. Science reveals uncomfortable truths about biology, mortality, and the indifference of the universe to human preferences. If students must be protected from all of this, they cannot be educated. They can only be kept comfortable.

The workplace version of this looks like conflict avoidance disguised as professionalism. Managers avoid giving honest feedback because they don't want employees to feel unsafe. Teams avoid necessary disagreements because someone might interpret pushback as hostility. Performance reviews become exercises in positive affirmation rather than honest assessment. The result is that problems fester, mediocrity becomes acceptable, and people never receive the information they need to improve—all in the name of safety.

Even parenting has been reshaped by this confusion. Parents hover over their children, ready to intervene at the first sign of difficulty. A child struggles with homework? The parent complains to the teacher rather than letting the child learn to ask for help. A child has a disagreement with a friend? The parent calls the other parent to mediate rather than letting the children work it out. A child faces disappointment? The parent rushes in to fix it rather than allowing the child to experience and recover from it.

What these children learn is not safety but dependency. They learn that discomfort is abnormal, that challenge is unfair, that they cannot trust themselves to handle difficulty. When they reach adulthood, they lack the psychological tools to navigate setbacks, criticism, or conflict—precisely because they were "protected" from developing those tools.

The strangest part of all this is that the expansion of safety language was driven, at least initially, by genuine compassion. People wanted to protect those who'd been harmed. They wanted to create environments where everyone could participate without fear. They wanted to acknowledge that words can wound, that some experiences genuinely traumatize, that not all harm is physical. These are reasonable concerns. The problem isn't the impulse to care; it's the loss of proportion.

When everything becomes a safety issue, nothing is. When *I feel unsafe* can mean anything from *someone threatened me* to *someone disagreed with me*, the phrase loses its power to alert us to real danger. It's the boy who cried wolf, translated into institutional policy.

Real danger still exists. Real trauma still occurs. Real threats still require real responses. But when institutions treat every claim of unsafety as equally valid, they lose the ability to distinguish between someone who's been assaulted and someone who's been challenged. Both get routed through the same bureaucratic process. Both are told their feelings are valid. But their situations are not equivalent and treating them as such helps neither.

Moreover, the language of safety gives enormous power to whoever invokes it. In the old understanding, you had to demonstrate actual danger—show the faulty wiring, point to the structural weakness, document the threat. In the new understanding, you merely have to claim that you feel unsafe. Your subjective experience becomes unchallengeable. And since feelings are invisible and unmeasurable, there's no way to verify or dispute them.

This creates perverse incentives. People learn that *I feel unsafe* is a trump card that ends discussions, gets policies changed, and removes people from positions. Whether the feeling corresponds to any objective reality becomes irrelevant. The claim itself is sufficient.

So how do we recover a meaningful understanding of safety?

Not the inflated version that treats every discomfort as danger, but the original version—the one that protected people from real harm while expecting them to develop the strength to handle everything else.

First, we have to restore the distinction between danger and discomfort.

They are not the same thing. Danger threatens your physical wellbeing or your fundamental rights. Discomfort challenges your assumptions, threatens your comfort, or makes you feel bad. The first requires intervention. The second requires resilience.

This distinction used to be obvious. A parent could tell the difference between a child who'd been physically hurt and a child who was upset about losing a game. A teacher could distinguish between a student being bullied and a student being challenged by difficult material. An employer could separate genuine workplace harassment from interpersonal friction. The categories were clear because the consequences were different.

But we've systematically blurred these lines until many people genuinely cannot tell the difference anymore. They experience intellectual challenge as assault. They interpret disagreement as violence. They treat hurt feelings as equivalent to physical injury. This isn't metaphor for them—they actually experience these things as indistinguishable. And once that conflation becomes complete, meaningful safety becomes impossible, because safety now means eliminating all negative emotion, which cannot be done.

The restoration of this distinction requires both cultural change and individual practice. Culturally, we need to stop validating every claim of harm as if subjective feeling were objective fact. When someone says "I feel unsafe," the appropriate response is not automatic accommodation but honest inquiry: What specifically makes you feel that way? Is there an objective threat, or are you uncomfortable? If you're uncomfortable, is that necessarily bad?

These questions aren't hostile—they're necessary. A person who feels unsafe walking through a dark parking lot at night is experiencing appropriate threat assessment. A person who feels unsafe sitting in a classroom where someone disagrees with them is experiencing discomfort, not danger. Treating both situations identically helps neither person. The first needs better lighting or a security escort. The second needs to develop emotional regulation and intellectual courage.

Consider what this looks like in practice. A college student goes to her dean and says she feels unsafe because a professor assigned a book that contains racial slurs in its historical dialogue. The dean has two options. Option one: remove the book from the syllabus, validate her feeling as legitimate harm, and reinforce the idea that encountering difficult material is dangerous. Option two: acknowledge her discomfort, explain the educational value of engaging with historical texts even when they're disturbing, and help her develop the skills to process challenging content without experiencing it as threat.

The first option is easier. It avoids conflict. It makes the student feel heard and protected. But it teaches her that discomfort equals danger and that the appropriate response to discomfort is avoidance. It prepares her for a world that doesn't exist—one where she'll never encounter ideas that upset her.

The second option is harder. It requires the dean to hold the line between genuine protection and enabling fragility. It asks the student to do difficult emotional work. But it teaches her that she's capable of encountering disturbing material and thinking through it, that discomfort is survivable, that intellectual growth often requires emotional discomfort. It prepares her for the actual world, where difficult ideas are everywhere and avoidance isn't possible.

The same principle applies everywhere. A workplace conflict isn't automatically harassment just because someone feels bad. A disagreement isn't automatically hostile just because it creates tension. A child's disappointment isn't automatically unfair just because it hurts. Learning to calibrate our responses to actual threat level rather than emotional intensity is essential for both individual wellbeing and functional institutions.

This doesn't mean discomfort doesn't matter. It means discomfort is often the sign that growth is possible. A muscle that's never stressed doesn't grow stronger. A mind that's never challenged doesn't grow deeper. A person who's never faced difficulty doesn't develop competence. Discomfort is the friction that produces capability.

When we protect people from all discomfort in the name of safety, we're not making them safer—we're making them weaker. We're teaching them that they're fragile, that the world is full of threats, that they need constant protection. And ironically, this makes them less safe, because they never develop the judgment to distinguish real threats from imagined ones.

Second, we have to rebuild resilience as a cultural expectation.

Resilience isn't callousness. It's not indifference to suffering. It's the capacity to encounter hardship and recover from it. People are far more resilient than our current culture assumes. But resilience, like any capacity, must be practiced. You don't develop it by avoiding difficulty; you develop it by facing difficulty in measured doses and learning that you can survive it.

The psychological research on this is unambiguous. Post-traumatic growth is real—many people who experience severe hardship don't just recover; they become stronger, more capable, more psychologically robust than they were before. But this only happens if they're given the opportunity to process the experience and discover their own capacity to handle it. If they're instead taught that they've been irreparably damaged, that they need perpetual accommodation, that they should identify primarily as victims, they often remain fragile indefinitely.

This principle applies not just to trauma but to ordinary difficulty. Children who are allowed to struggle with hard problems develop better problem-solving skills than children who are immediately helped. Students who receive honest feedback, even when it stings, improve faster than students who receive only praise. Employees who have to navigate workplace conflicts develop better interpersonal skills than employees who are shielded from all friction. In each case, the temporary discomfort produces lasting capability.

But our current approach to safety systematically prevents this development. We've created what psychologists Jonathon Haidt and Greg Lukianoff call "safetyism"—the belief that people are inherently fragile and must be protected from anything that might cause distress (*The Coddling of the American Mind*). This isn't supported by evidence about human psychology. It's a cultural assumption, and it's a destructive one.

Consider what happens in schools that have fully embraced safetyism. Students are protected from competitive games, difficult grading, challenging reading, and disagreeable classmates. Every potential source of stress is eliminated or softened. The assumption is that this creates better mental health outcomes. But the opposite occurs. Anxiety and depression rates in these environments are higher, not lower. Why? Because students never learn that they can handle difficulty. They never develop the confidence that comes from facing a challenge and overcoming it. They remain perpetually fragile because they've been perpetually protected.

Now consider an alternative approach. A school that takes resilience seriously doesn't eliminate all challenge—it provides appropriately challenging experiences in contexts where students have support. They assign difficult books but discuss them thoughtfully. They maintain academic standards but provide resources for struggling students. They allow competitive activities but teach good sportsmanship. They let students experience failure but help them learn from it. The message is consistent: you are capable, difficulty is normal, and struggling doesn't mean you're broken—it means you're learning.

The students who emerge from these environments are measurably more resilient. Not because they've had easier lives, but because they've had practice handling difficulty. They've learned that discomfort is temporary, that failure isn't permanent, that they possess internal resources for handling challenges. This is real safety—not protection from all hardship, but confidence in one's ability to handle hardship.

Rebuilding resilience as a cultural expectation means several things practically. It means parents letting children experience natural consequences instead of perpetually intervening. When a child forgets their homework, the consequence is a bad grade, not the parent rushing it to school. When a child has a conflict with a friend, the response is coaching them through it, not calling the other parent to fix it. When a child faces disappointment, the message is "you can handle this," not "this is unfair and we'll make it go away."

It means teachers maintaining academic standards and giving honest feedback. A paper that's poorly reasoned should receive a low grade and specific criticism about how to improve. A student who's struggling should receive support but not grade inflation. A classroom discussion should allow for genuine disagreement, even when it creates temporary discomfort. The goal is learning, not comfort, and learning often requires discomfort.

It means employers giving real performance feedback. The employee who's underperforming needs to hear it directly, with specific examples and clear expectations for improvement. The team that's avoiding a necessary conflict needs to be pushed to address it. The workplace that's functional isn't one where everyone always feels comfortable—it's one where people trust each other enough to be honest, even when honesty creates friction.

Most importantly, it means expecting adults to manage their own emotional responses. We've created a culture where emotional fragility is honored, where claiming distress gives you power, where managing your own reactions is seen as an unfair burden. But emotional self-regulation is a basic adult skill. It's not optional, and it's not oppressive to expect it. The person who cannot hear criticism without experiencing it as attack, who cannot encounter disagreement without experiencing it as assault, who cannot handle disappointment without experiencing it as trauma, is not demonstrating sensitivity—they're demonstrating a lack of basic psychological resilience that will harm them throughout their life.

Recovering resilience means recovering the expectation that adults should be able to handle difficulty without institutional intervention. It means praising strength rather than fragility. It means recognizing that the goal isn't to eliminate all discomfort from life—it's to build people capable of enduring discomfort without collapsing. It means understanding that you do someone no favors by protecting them from every challenge. You only prepare them for failure.

Third, we have to recover honest risk assessment.

Not every playground needs to be padded. Not every book needs a trigger warning. Not every disagreement needs HR mediation. Real safety professionals understand that you can't eliminate all risk—you can only mitigate the risks that matter most. The goal isn't zero risk; it's intelligent risk management. And intelligent risk management requires distinguishing between risks worth worrying about and risks worth accepting.

In engineering, this distinction is foundational. Engineers don't try to make bridges that can never fail under any circumstance—that would be impossible and economically absurd. Instead, they design for specific load tolerances with appropriate safety margins. They identify the most likely failure modes and design against those. They accept that some vanishingly small risk always remains, because eliminating all risk would mean building nothing.

The same principle applies to everyday safety, but we've lost sight of it. We've become a culture that demands zero risk, treats every potential harm as equally serious, and cannot distinguish between precautions that matter and precautions that don't.

Again, consider playground safety. Obviously, playgrounds should be reasonably safe—equipment should be sturdy, surfaces should cushion falls, heights should be appropriate for the age group. But there's a difference between reasonable precaution and eliminating all possibility of injury. A playground where no child can ever get hurt is also a playground where no child can develop physical confidence, learn to assess risk, or experience the minor feedback that teaches caution.

Studies of playground safety have found something counterintuitive: when playgrounds are made completely safe, injury rates don't drop to zero—they sometimes increase. Why? Because children don't learn to assess risk accurately. They attempt things they're not ready for because they've never experienced the minor consequences that teach judgment. They don't develop the physical skills that come from navigating actual challenges. The "safe" playground produces children who are less safe in every other context.

The same pattern shows up everywhere. Schools that eliminate all competitive activities don't produce students with higher self-esteem—they produce students who've never learned to handle losing. Workplaces that mediate every interpersonal friction don't produce better teams—they produce teams that can't function without constant management oversight. Families that shield children from every disappointment don't produce confident adults—they produce adults who fall apart at the first serious setback.

Honest risk assessment requires asking: What is the actual probability of harm? How severe would the harm be? What capability do we lose by eliminating the risk? Is the protection worth the cost?

Take trigger warnings as an example. The original intent was narrow: warn students before showing graphic visual content that might genuinely re-traumatize survivors of violence. That's reasonable risk management. The risk (re-traumatization) is real but rare, the severity is high, and the cost of the warning is negligible.

But trigger warnings expanded to cover virtually any content someone might find upsetting. Professors are now expected to warn students before discussing historical racism, before assigning novels with sad endings, before showing films that depict violence, before reading poetry about death. At this point, the warnings aren't managing real risk—they're managing discomfort. And the cost is no longer negligible: students learn to avoid difficulty rather than engage with it, education is constrained by the need to protect feelings, and the signal value of warnings is diluted until they're meaningless.

Honest risk assessment would distinguish between these cases. Content that might genuinely re-traumatize someone who's recently experienced sexual assault? Reasonable to warn. Content that might make someone uncomfortable because it challenges their political beliefs or makes them sad? That's what education does. No warning needed.

The same logic applies to parenting. A parent who doesn't let their teenager drive until they've had proper training is managing risk intelligently. A parent who doesn't let their teenager walk to school alone at age sixteen is not managing risk—they're preventing normal development. The first is responding to actual danger with appropriate precaution. The second is responding to imagined danger with harmful overprotection.

Recovering honest risk assessment means recovering the ability to distinguish between real threats and imagined ones, between reasonable precaution and paranoid avoidance, between protection that helps and protection that harms. It means accepting that life contains risk, that some risk is worth taking, and that eliminating all risk isn't possible or desirable.

It also means recovering institutional courage. Many of the most excessive safety measures aren't imposed because anyone believes they're necessary—they're imposed because institutions are afraid of liability, criticism, or controversy. A school doesn't remove its playground equipment because they genuinely believe children will be seriously injured; they remove it because they're afraid of lawsuits. A university doesn't cancel a speaker because they genuinely believe students are in danger; they cancel because they're afraid of protests.

This institutional cowardice, dressed up as safety concern, is corrosive. It teaches everyone involved that authorities don't believe in their own stated values, that risk avoidance matters more than growth or learning, that the squeaky wheel gets the grease even when the squeaky wheel is wrong. Recovering honest risk assessment requires recovering the courage to say: this isn't actually dangerous, the discomfort is acceptable, we're not going to eliminate every possible negative outcome because doing so would eliminate the positive outcomes too.

Fourth, we have to stop treating feelings as evidence.

"I feel unsafe" is important information about someone's internal state. But it's not necessarily accurate information about external reality. A person can feel unsafe in a perfectly safe environment because of their own anxiety, past trauma, or misinterpretation. Their feeling is real, but that doesn't mean the environment is dangerous. The appropriate response is not to reshape the environment but to help the person develop more accurate threat assessment.

This principle runs counter to everything our culture has been teaching for the last two decades. We've elevated subjective feeling to supreme authority. *Your truth* has replaced *the truth*. *Lived experience* is treated as unquestionable. *I feel* statements are given automatic credibility that *I think* statements aren't. The underlying assumption is that feelings are always valid and should always be honored.

But this assumption is false, and honoring it causes harm. Feelings are real in the sense that people genuinely experience them. But feelings are not always accurate guides to reality. A person with social anxiety might feel unsafe in a crowded room even though no threat exists. A person with past trauma might feel unsafe hearing certain words even though the words themselves pose no danger. A person with confirmation bias might feel unsafe around people who disagree with them even though disagreement isn't threat.

In each case, the feeling is real, but the appropriate response is not to validate the feeling as accurate. The appropriate response is to help the person distinguish between their internal state and external reality, to develop better threat assessment, to learn that they can tolerate the situation even though it's uncomfortable.

This is actually the foundation of effective therapy for anxiety disorders. Cognitive Behavioral Therapy doesn't tell patients that their feelings of danger are accurate. It helps them recognize that their threat assessment is mis calibrated, that they're experiencing anxiety in situations that aren't actually dangerous, and that they can learn to tolerate the discomfort until their nervous system recalibrates. The goal isn't to eliminate all situations that trigger anxiety—it's to help the person function despite anxiety.

But our broader culture has taken exactly the opposite approach. Instead of helping people recalibrate inaccurate threat assessment, we validate it. Instead of building tolerance for discomfort, we eliminate sources of discomfort. Instead of teaching people to examine whether their feelings correspond to reality, we teach them that their feelings are reality.

Consider what this looks like on a college campus. A student reports feeling unsafe because a professor assigned a reading that challenged her political beliefs. Under the therapeutic model, a counselor would help her understand that intellectual challenge isn't danger, that discomfort is a normal part of learning, that she can engage with ideas she disagrees with without being harmed. The goal would be helping her develop intellectual resilience.

Under the current campus culture model, administrators validate her feeling of unsafety as accurate, the professor is pressured to remove the reading or offer alternatives, and the student learns that her subjective discomfort is sufficient reason to change institutional policy. The goal is eliminating her discomfort rather than building her capability.

The second approach isn't compassionate—it's disabling. It teaches the student that she cannot handle disagreement, that authority figures will protect her from challenge, that her subjective feelings should override everyone else's interest in robust intellectual inquiry. It prepares her for failure in any environment that hasn't been specifically engineered around her sensitivities.

Stopping the treatment of feelings as evidence requires institutional courage and cultural change. It means administrators saying, "I understand you feel unsafe, but no threat exists, and we're not going to change policy based on subjective discomfort." It means therapists helping clients distinguish between feeling and reality rather than validating all feelings as equally accurate. It means parents teaching children that feeling scared or upset doesn't necessarily mean something is wrong.

This isn't invalidation of feelings—it's appropriate contextualization of them. Your feelings matter as information about your internal state. But they don't automatically override other considerations. The person who feels unsafe in every situation that makes them uncomfortable needs help developing better threat assessment, not a world reshaped to eliminate all discomfort.

The alternative—treating every claim of feeling unsafe as automatically accurate—makes genuine safety impossible. If any subjective claim of harm must be accepted without scrutiny, then the most sensitive person in any group determines what everyone can do or say. The capacity to claim harm becomes a form of power, and people learn to weaponize their sensitivity. This helps no one. It doesn't make environments genuinely safer. It just makes them more controlled by whoever has the most fragile nervous system or the least scrupulous willingness to claim harm.

Finally, we have to remember that true safety doesn't mean protection from all harm.

It means having the tools, knowledge, and resilience to navigate a world that contains harm. The goal isn't to create a world where nothing bad ever happens—that's impossible. The goal is to create people who can handle difficulty when it inevitably arrives.

This understanding used to be foundational to how we raised children, educated students, and structured workplaces. The assumption was that the world contained genuine challenges and dangers, and that the task of preparation was to build capable people, not to create perfectly safe environments.

Parents didn't try to eliminate all risk from their children's lives—they tried to teach their children to assess and manage risk. They let children climb trees, knowing they might fall, because learning to climb safely was more important than preventing all falls. They let children walk to school, knowing theoretical dangers existed, because developing independence and spatial and situational awareness mattered more than eliminating all possibility of harm.

Schools didn't try to protect students from all difficult content—they tried to teach students to engage with difficulty thoughtfully. They assigned challenging books, including ones with disturbing content, because learning to process difficult material was part of education. They maintained academic standards that some students wouldn't meet, because learning to handle failure and work harder was part of growing up.

Workplaces didn't try to eliminate all interpersonal friction—they expected adults to navigate normal workplace relationships. They gave honest performance feedback, even when it was uncomfortable. They allowed disagreement and debate. They assumed that people could handle the ordinary difficulties of working with others.

All of this was based on a simple principle: safety isn't about eliminating exposure to all difficulty. It's about building people who are capable of handling difficulty. The protected life doesn't produce strong people. The challenged life does—provided the challenges are appropriate to the person's developmental level and they have support in meeting them.

This is what makes the playground metaphor so apt. The old playground had real risks—you could fall from the monkey bars, you could get hurt on the seesaw, you could skin your knee on the gravel. Children got hurt regularly. But they also learned physical confidence, risk assessment, and resilience. They developed the judgment to know which challenges they were ready for and which they weren't.

The new playground eliminates these risks through padding, low heights, and soft materials. Children don't get hurt as often—at least not on the playground itself. But they don't develop physical confidence or risk assessment either. And when they encounter real danger in other contexts—riding bikes, climbing rocks, playing sports—they're less prepared, not more.

The goal should be appropriate challenge with appropriate support. Children need playgrounds that let them test their limits without being genuinely dangerous. Students need exposure to difficult ideas with guidance in how to engage with them. Employees need honest feedback with support in improving. In each case, the safety comes not from eliminating difficulty but from building capability to handle it.

This requires a fundamental shift in how we think about protection. Protection isn't keeping people in bubbles where nothing can touch them. Protection is giving them the tools they need to face the world and trust themselves to navigate it. It's not promising that nothing will ever go wrong. It's promising that when things do go wrong—and they will—they'll have the resilience to recover.

Real safety creates the conditions for courage. It gives people confidence in their own capacity. It teaches them that they can handle disappointment, process difficulty, recover from setbacks. It doesn't pretend the world is safe in some absolute sense—it prepares people for the world as it actually is.

And that preparation is the only real safety that exists. Because the world will not be redesigned around anyone's sensitivities. Reality does not accommodate feelings. Physics doesn't care about your comfort level. Other people will continue having different views, and some of them will express those views in ways you find offensive. Disappointment, failure, loss, and difficulty are not glitches in the system—they're built into the human condition.

The question is whether we prepare people to handle that reality or whether we pretend we can protect them from it. The first approach produces capable adults. The second produces permanent children who collapse the first time reality asserts itself.

Flannery O'Connor's line remains sharp: "The truth does not change according to our ability to stomach it."

The world is not *safe* in the way we've come to use that word. It never was, and it never will be. It contains real dangers—structural, biological, psychological. But it also contains challenges, friction, disagreement, and discomfort. Learning to distinguish between the two is one of the central tasks of adulthood.

The children who grow up on risk-free playgrounds don't learn safety—they learn fearlessness in dangerous contexts and fear in safe ones. The students who are protected from challenging ideas don't learn to think—they learn that thinking is dangerous. The employees who never receive honest feedback don't learn to improve—they learn that honesty is hostile.

Safety culture, paradoxically, makes us less safe. It produces people who cannot assess risk accurately, who overreact to minor threats and underreact to major ones, who demand protection from challenges they should be learning to overcome.

The solution isn't to abandon care or revert to callousness. It's to rebuild the distinction between protection and coddling, between reasonable precaution and pathological avoidance, between safety that strengthens and safety that weakens.

Real safety creates the conditions for courage. It gives people the tools they need to face the world and trust themselves to navigate it. It doesn't promise that nothing will ever go wrong. It promises that when things do go wrong—and they will—you'll have the resilience to recover.

That's the kind of safety worth building.

And it begins the moment we stop pretending that discomfort and danger are the same thing.

FOUR

COURAGE

Courage is not simply one of the virtues, but the form of every virtue at the testing point.
—C.S. Lewis

In structural engineering, they talk about structural integrity—whether something can bear the load it's designed to carry. Courage used to have structural integrity. It meant bearing a specific kind of load: real danger, undertaken willingly, for something beyond yourself. The word could carry weight because everyone understood what it was for. Now courage has been asked to carry loads it was never designed for. We use it for emotional discomfort, social awkwardness, personal authenticity. And like any structure bearing more weight than it was built for, the word is failing.

Courage used to mean something precise. It was the willingness to face genuine danger—physical, social, or professional—for the sake of something that mattered more than your own safety. The danger had to be real. The choice had to be free. And the motive had to be something larger than self-interest.

A soldier advancing under fire showed courage. A whistleblower risking their career to expose corruption showed courage. A parent shielding their child from an attacker showed courage. The common thread wasn't just difficulty—it was danger. Real cost. The possibility of serious loss.

That understanding has dissolved. Courage has been democratized, sentimentalized, turned into a participation trophy for anything that feels hard. We now call it courage to post on social media, to "be yourself," to express your feelings, to ask for what you need. These might be good things—honesty, authenticity, self-advocacy all have value—but they're not *courage*. Courage isn't about doing what's emotionally difficult. It's about doing what's dangerous when something important requires it.

The shift happened gradually, through several cultural changes that each seemed reasonable but collectively gutted the word. Therapeutic culture had already redefined discomfort as danger—that same confusion now inflated courage beyond recognition, turning vulnerability into the new bravery and any act of self-disclosure into a courageous act.

First, identity politics made "being yourself" into an act of resistance. For people whose identities have been marginalized or attacked, visibility can carry real risk. Admitting that you're different in a hostile environment takes courage. Living openly when doing so invites violence takes courage. But the language of courage spread to contexts where no risk existed. "It's so courageous of you to be yourself" became a standard affirmation—even in environments specifically designed to celebrate exactly that identity, even when being yourself brought applause rather than danger.

Second, and more corrosively, we lost sight of what courage actually looks like when it fails. It doesn't fail dramatically. It fails quietly, in institutional life, in the daily choices of people who know exactly what the right thing is—and choose silence anyway. The engineer who knows the design is flawed but says nothing because the project is behind schedule. The physician who suspects a colleague is impaired but doesn't report it because of the professional fallout. The manager who watches someone being treated unjustly in a meeting but stays quiet because the person doing it is powerful. These aren't failures of perception. Everyone in the room knows what's happening. The cost of speaking is real and understood. And the silence is chosen.

That's what courage looks like when it fails—not theatrical cowardice, not someone trembling and running away, but the quiet calculation that this particular moment isn't worth it. The slow accumulation of those calculations is how institutions rot. Not through dramatic failure but through the habitual small surrenders of people who knew better and said nothing.

The result is that courage now describes almost any action that makes you feel uncomfortable. Speaking up in a meeting where you're nervous. Wearing an outfit that doesn't conform to expectations. Admitting you were wrong. Asking for help. Setting boundaries. These might be healthy, mature, or wise—but they're not courageous unless something is genuinely at stake.

Consider the difference between two acts, both called courageous in contemporary language.

In 1955, Rosa Parks refused to give up her seat on a Montgomery bus. She knew what would happen—arrest, public vilification, threats to her safety and livelihood. She did it anyway because the indignity of segregation mattered more than her personal safety. That's courage—clear, costly, chosen.

In 2023, a college student posted on social media about their journey with anxiety and depression. The post received thousands of likes, supportive comments, and shares. Campus counseling services reached out to offer support. The student was invited to speak at a mental health awareness event. News outlets featured their story as an example of "courageous vulnerability."

Both acts might be valuable. Parks's refusal sparked a movement. The student's post might have helped others feel less alone. But only one involved actual danger. Only one required choosing a costly path when a safe one was available. Only one is courage in the original sense of the word.

The problem isn't that we're honoring the student—the problem is that we're using the same word for both acts. When courage describes both facing arrest for civil rights and posting about your feelings to a supportive audience, the word has lost its ability to mark the distinction between safety and danger, between risk and reward, between what costs you something and what costs you nothing.

The pattern repeats. The celebrity who "courageously" comes out as gay in an industry where being gay is celebrated isn't showing courage—they're making a safe choice that will likely enhance their career. The person who stays in the closet in a genuinely hostile environment and then finally speaks up is showing courage. But we apply the word to the first case and often ignore the second.

Or consider the corporate executive who gives a speech about the importance of "having the courage to fail." They're not talking about actual danger. They're talking about trying new strategies that might not work. Failure in this context means a project doesn't succeed, not that anyone gets hurt. It's risk in the sense of uncertainty, not risk in the sense of danger. But calling it courage makes the executive sound bold, even though nothing is really at stake for them personally.

The inflation of courage creates several problems.

First, it makes actual courage harder to recognize. When everything from posting on Instagram to wearing unconventional clothes gets called courageous, we lose the ability to distinguish these acts from someone running into a burning building or standing up to violent threats. The word becomes praise rather than description. And when courage is just another way of saying "good job," it stops meaning anything specific.

Second, it creates perverse incentives. If courage is defined as doing what feels emotionally difficult, then people will start performing difficulty. They'll treat minor acts as major sacrifices. They'll inflate the risk they're facing to claim the status that comes with courage. Social media accelerates this—everyone competing to be the most vulnerable, the most authentic, the most brave, even when no actual danger exists.

Third, it devalues real courage. The father who jumped into a riptide to save his drowning child and the person who posted about their therapy journey both get called courageous. But these aren't equivalent acts. One risked death. The other risked nothing. When we use the same word for both, we're not honoring the person who shared their feelings—we're dishonoring the person who risked his life.

Fourth, it produces a culture that can't identify when courage is actually needed. If posting your feelings is courage, what do you call the person who stands alone against injustice? If "being yourself" is courage, what do you call the person who sacrifices their safety for someone else? We've spent the word on easy things, so we have nothing left for hard ones.

The person who faces actual danger doesn't usually call themselves courageous. They do what needs doing and move on. Courage, in its real form, doesn't announce itself. It doesn't perform for an audience. It shows up when required and disappears when the crisis passes. This modesty is part of what makes it courage—it's not done for recognition.

I served in the military as an aircraft mechanic. I wasn't in combat. I didn't face enemy fire. I did my job—important work, sometimes under uncomfortable conditions, but not dangerous work. I wasn't courageous just for wearing the uniform.

But I have known, or known of, people who were. The pilots who flew missions knowing the equipment might fail. The Seabee who approached unexploded ordnance. The medics who ran toward gunfire to reach wounded soldiers. They didn't talk about their courage. Most of them would be uncomfortable being called courageous. They'd say they were just doing their job, that anyone would have done the same, that the real heroes were the ones who didn't make it back.

That reluctance to claim courage is itself part of what makes it real. Because courage isn't a performance—it's a response. It's what happens when someone is confronted with danger and chooses to face it anyway, not for recognition, but because something important requires it. The moment you're doing it to be called courageous, it stops being courage. It becomes something else—performance, status-seeking, image management.

But in a culture where courage has been inflated, this modesty becomes invisible. The quiet acts of real bravery go unnoticed because they're not performing courage—they're just doing it. Meanwhile, the loud performances of pseudo-courage get celebrated precisely because they're loud.

Engineering has its own version of this moment. I've been in rooms where the numbers didn't support the decision that was already being made—where someone needed a finding to come out a certain way for reasons that had nothing to do with the engineering. Those moments don't require physical courage. But they require something that functions the same way: the willingness to say what's true when saying it carries a cost. When speaking up might mean being sidelined, labeled as difficult, or losing a relationship with someone whose approval you valued.

I won't pretend I always got those moments right. But I learned something about courage from them that no classroom ever taught me: courage isn't the absence of fear. It's the recognition that something—the integrity of the work, the safety of the people depending on it, the simple fact that it's true—matters more than whatever it will cost you to say so.

C.S. Lewis understood that courage isn't a standalone virtue—it's what allows you to practice other virtues when doing so is dangerous. You can't be honest when honesty is costly unless you have courage. You can't pursue justice when pursuing it threatens you unless you have courage. You can't love sacrificially unless you have courage. Courage is what lets all other virtues exist under pressure.

This is why Lewis called courage *"the form of every virtue at the testing point."* He wasn't saying courage is more important than other virtues—he was saying it's what makes other virtues possible when they become costly. Anyone can be honest when honesty is safe. Anyone can be kind when kindness costs nothing. Anyone can stand for justice when justice is popular. Courage is what lets you keep practicing virtue when practicing it puts you at risk.

Without courage, every other virtue becomes conditional. You'll be honest unless it's dangerous. You'll be just unless it costs you something. You'll be loving unless it requires sacrifice. Courage removes the "unless." It's the virtue that protects all other virtues from collapsing under pressure.

This is also why courage has to remain rare and costly in its definition. If courage just means doing what feels difficult, then it's no longer protecting virtue under pressure—it's just describing everyday discomfort. And everyday discomfort doesn't threaten virtue. Danger does. Social cost does. Professional risk does. Physical threat does.

The person who tells the truth when lying would save their career is exercising courage. The person who tells the truth when it's emotionally difficult but socially safe is exercising honesty. Both are good. But they're not the same. The first requires courage because a real cost is involved. The second doesn't.

When we lose this distinction, we lose our ability to identify the moments when courage is actually needed. And those moments still come. Not often, not to everyone, but they come. And when they do—when honesty will cost you your job, when justice will cost you your reputation, when doing what's right will cost you your safety—you need to know what you're being asked for. You need to recognize that this is courage territory, that the cost is real, and that paying it anyway is what courage has always meant.

This is why the degradation of the word matters so much. When courage becomes just another word for self-expression or emotional openness, we lose the thing that makes costly virtue possible. We lose the language for the moment when someone has to choose between what's right and what's safe—and chooses right.

So how do we recover courage?

First, we have to restore the distinction between danger and discomfort. Discomfort is what you feel when something is awkward, vulnerable, or socially risky. Danger is what you face when something could genuinely harm you—physically, professionally, relationally. Courage applies to danger, not discomfort. We need other words for discomfort: honesty, vulnerability, authenticity, openness. These are good things, but they're not courage.

Second, we have to stop using courage as a term of affirmation. When someone does something difficult, we can appreciate it without calling it courageous. "That took honesty" or "That was vulnerable" or "I respect that choice" all work fine. We don't need to escalate every good act into courage. Courage should be reserved for the moments when it actually applies—when someone is facing real danger and chooses to continue forward anyway.

Third, we have to recognize that courage often looks ordinary. The person who quietly reports misconduct knowing it will cost them their job is showing courage. The parent who confronts their child's abuser is showing courage. The employee who refuses to participate in something unethical despite pressure from superiors is showing courage. These acts don't always look dramatic. They often look like someone doing what's necessary and then going back to their regular life. But they involve real risk, and that's what makes them courageous.

Fourth, we have to remember that courage is instrumental, not terminal. You're not courageous for its own sake—you're courageous in service of something else. The soldier isn't courageous just to be brave; they're courageous to protect others. The whistleblower isn't courageous for the thrill; they're courageous because truth matters. Courage without purpose is just recklessness. Courage with purpose is virtue.

This means recovering courage starts with recovering the things worth being courageous for. If nothing matters enough to risk something over, courage becomes impossible. But if truth matters, if justice matters, if protecting others matters—then courage becomes the natural response when those things are threatened.

The contemporary problem isn't that people lack the capacity for courage. It's that we've been trained to believe nothing is worth the risk. We've been taught that the highest good is safety, comfort, and self-preservation. We've been told that any cost to those goods is too high. And in that framework, courage looks like foolishness.

But courage has never been about safety. It's about recognizing that some things matter more than safety. That some truths are worth telling even when telling them is dangerous. That some people are worth protecting even when protecting them puts you at risk. That some principles are worth standing for even when standing for them costs you something real.

Recovering courage, then, means recovering the hierarchy of goods. Safety isn't nothing—it matters. But it's not everything. It's not the highest good. And when it's treated as the highest good, courage becomes impossible, because courage by definition means accepting danger for something you value more than safety.

Finally, we have to accept that most of us will go through life without facing moments that require real courage—and that's fine. Courage is rare because dangerous situations requiring a choice are rare. Most people will live good, decent lives without ever needing to be courageous. That's not a moral failing. That's just the texture of an ordinary life in a reasonably stable society.

But when those moments do come—when something dangerous must be faced, when safety and duty conflict, when doing what's right will cost you something real—we need a word that can name what happens when someone steps forward anyway.

We need the word *courage* to mean what it always meant: not the willingness to feel uncomfortable, but the willingness to face danger for something that matters more than safety. And if we've spent the word on smaller things, it won't be there when we need it.

Courage isn't common. It's not supposed to be. It's the exception that proves human beings are capable of rising above self-preservation when something important enough requires it. That capacity is worth preserving. And the word that names it is worth guarding.

Because someday—maybe not today, maybe not in your lifetime, but someday—someone will face a moment when courage is needed. And when that moment comes, we'll need a word that hasn't been thinned by overuse, a word that still carries the weight of actual danger and actual choice and actual sacrifice.

We'll need the word courage to be there, sharp and ready, naming what it's always named: the willingness to face what's dangerous because something more important than safety is at stake.

FIVE

HERO

Courage is found in unlikely places.
—J.R.R. Tolkien

In March 2020, as hospitals filled and the world locked down, a peculiar phrase appeared on signs across America: "Healthcare Heroes." It showed up on storefronts, billboards, homemade posters taped to apartment windows. People banged pots and pans at 7 PM to applaud nurses finishing shifts. The sentiment was genuine—gratitude for those working through danger when most of you stayed home.

But within weeks, the language expanded. "Essential workers" became heroes. Grocery clerks, delivery drivers, warehouse employees—anyone whose job required them to leave the house. Then it spread further. Teachers working from home became heroes. Parents homeschooling their children became heroes. People staying home and doing nothing became heroes for "flattening the curve."

By summer, the word had lost all shape. A hero was anyone doing anything that felt even mildly inconvenient. The term that once described someone who voluntarily risked themselves for others now applied to nearly everyone simply for continuing to exist during difficult circumstances.

This wasn't a pandemic phenomenon. It was the acceleration of something that had been happening for years. The word *hero* had been inflating for decades, expanding to cover more and more territory until it no longer meant anything specific at all.

That's what happens when a culture loses its sense of moral altitude.

The word *hero* used to carry weight because it named something rare and costly. A hero was someone who stepped forward when others stepped back. Someone who accepted danger on behalf of others. Someone who made a sacrifice—of safety, comfort, or life itself—for a cause or person beyond themselves.

Heroism wasn't about being good at your job. It wasn't about surviving hardship. It wasn't about being visible or admired. It was about a specific moral structure: voluntary risk undertaken for the sake of another. The risk had to be real. The decision had to be free. And the motive had to be something larger than self-interest.

By that standard, heroism was uncommon. Most people lived ordinary, decent lives without ever facing a moment that called for it. And that was fine. Heroism wasn't supposed to be common. It was the exception that reminded everyone of what human beings were capable of when the stakes were highest.

But something changed. Gradually, quietly, we began using heroic language for things that were admirable but not sacrificial. We called athletes heroes for winning games. We called celebrities heroes for speaking about their struggles. We called survivors heroes simply for enduring what they had no choice but to endure. The word became a term of general approval rather than a description of a specific kind of action.

The shift wasn't malicious. It came from good impulses—wanting to honor people, wanting to express gratitude, wanting to recognize effort. But good impulses, without precision, produce confusion. And once "hero" became a synonym for "anyone we appreciate," it stopped being able to name the thing it was meant to name.

Here's what the inflation looks like in practice.

A soldier throws himself on a grenade to save his squad. That's heroism—clear, unambiguous, costly. He chose to accept certain death to save others. The decision was voluntary. The risk was absolute. The motive was his brothers' lives, not his own benefit.

I was in the military. I was an aircraft mechanic. I did my job, went where I was told, did what I was told. Just wearing the uniform didn't make me a hero. It made me a servicemember doing what I'd signed up to do. That deserves respect—*but not the word hero.*

A teacher stays late after school to help a struggling student. That's admirable. It's generous. It's exactly what good teachers do. But it's not heroic. There's no danger. There's no sacrifice beyond inconvenience. It's good work done well, worthy of respect— *but not the word hero.*

A cancer patient undergoes chemotherapy. That's scary. That's resilience. That's endurance in the face of suffering. But it's not heroism. The patient isn't choosing risk on behalf of someone else—they're enduring risk imposed on them by circumstance. Survival isn't sacrifice.

A celebrity speaks publicly about their mental health struggles. That might help others feel less alone. It might reduce stigma. But it's not heroism. The celebrity faces no physical danger. The disclosure, while vulnerable, often increases their public standing and career prospects. There's no sacrifice—often there's reward.

None of this diminishes the value of these actions. Teachers matter. Patients deserve compassion. Vulnerability can be helpful. But calling everything heroic means we no longer have a word for the soldier who sacrifices himself. When the teacher and the soldier are both heroes, the word stops distinguishing between someone who gave extra time and someone who gave his life.

The same pattern appears everywhere. We call frontline workers heroes, but we're usually describing people doing their jobs under difficult conditions—which is admirable but not the same as voluntary sacrifice. We call protesters heroes, but protesting is often safe (especially when the majority supports your cause) and rarely involves genuine personal cost. We call ourselves heroes for making it through hard times, but endurance, however difficult, isn't the same as self-sacrifice.

The confusion comes from conflating different kinds of goodness. There's moral goodness (doing the right thing), professional excellence (doing your job well), personal resilience (surviving hardship), and social courage (speaking unpopular truths). These are all valuable. But heroism is something more specific: it's the willingness to bear serious personal cost for the good of another.

When we lose that distinction, we lose our ability to recognize heroism when it actually appears. And we lose the language that calls people toward it.

Tolkien understood this. His heroes aren't glamorous. They're small, frightened, ordinary people who nonetheless step forward when the moment demands it. Frodo carrying the Ring isn't rewarded with fame—he's broken by the burden. Sam climbing Mount Doom isn't seeking glory—he's simply refusing to abandon his friend. Aragorn claiming the throne isn't triumphant—it's a duty he accepts because it was appointed to him from birth.

What makes them heroes isn't their strength or skill. It's their willingness to carry what they'd rather not carry, to face what they'd rather not face, because something larger than themselves requires it. The cost is real. The choice is free. The motive is love or duty, not self-interest.

That's the moral structure of heroism. And it's rare—not because people are selfish, but because most circumstances don't demand it. Most of life is lived in quieter registers. Most goodness is expressed in steadiness, faithfulness, kindness—virtues that don't require danger. That's not a failing. That's just the texture of ordinary life.

But when we call everyone a hero, we obscure that structure. We suggest that heroism is about effort, or visibility, or identity, or simply being appreciated. We imply that the title is democratically available to anyone who wants it. And in doing so, we drain the word of its power to name the thing it was meant to name.

The cost isn't just linguistic. When a culture loses the ability to recognize heroism, it loses the ability to cultivate it. Young people need to see examples of genuine sacrifice—not because they'll all be called to it, but because those examples shape their sense of what human beings can be. If every act is heroic, then no act seems especially worth emulating. Moral aspiration requires moral altitude. You can't climb toward something if everything is already at the summit.

There's also a strange cruelty in the inflation. Calling everyone a hero sounds generous, but it actually diminishes the people we're trying to honor. The nurse who works through exhaustion deserves recognition for dedication and skill—but if we call her a hero simply for doing her job well, we cheapen the word for the nurse who throws herself between an attacker and a patient. The person who rushes into traffic to pull a child from the street deserves the word—but not if we've already given it to everyone who showed up to work during a difficult season.

Real heroes don't usually call themselves heroes. They're often uncomfortable with the label. They did what the moment required, and they'd prefer not to make much of it. That humility is part of what makes their actions heroic—they didn't do it for recognition. But when we use the word indiscriminately, we create a culture where everyone expects to be called a hero, where recognition becomes the point rather than the incidental result.

So how do we recover the word?

First, we reserve it. Not every good deed is heroic. Not every hard job is heroic. Not every act of endurance is heroic. This means developing vocabulary for other kinds of goodness—dedication, resilience, courage, generosity, professionalism, kindness.

What this looks like in practice: When a nurse works a double shift during a staffing crisis, we thank her for her dedication and competence. We make sure she's fairly compensated. We respect her professionalism. But we don't call her a hero—unless she does something beyond her job description, something that involves genuine sacrifice for another person's sake. And when we make that distinction, we honor both kinds of goodness appropriately. The nurse isn't diminished by accurate language. She's respected for what she actually did.

Second, we restore the elements that make heroism heroic: danger, choice, and sacrifice for another. All three must be present. If those elements aren't there, we're describing something else—something that might be admirable or courageous or generous, but not heroic.

What this looks like: The bystander who jumps into a river to save a drowning stranger is a hero—there's danger, there's choice (no one would blame him for calling 911 instead), and there's sacrifice (he's risking his life for someone he's never met). The lifeguard who pulls someone from the water during his shift is a trained professional doing his job well. Both deserve respect. Only one is doing something *heroic*. And if we can't tell the difference, we can't honor either one appropriately.

Third, we accept that heroism is supposed to be rare. It's the exception, not the norm. Most people will live good, decent lives without ever facing a moment that calls for heroism. That's not a disappointment—it's a sign that their circumstances didn't demand it.

What this looks like: We stop treating the absence of heroism as a moral failure. The person who never confronts an armed attacker or never has to choose between their safety and someone else's life hasn't failed at anything. They've simply lived an ordinary life—which is what most lives are and should be. Heroism matters precisely because it's rare. Common things don't require uncommon words.

Fourth, we stop using *hero* as a term of affection or appreciation. If we want the word to mean something, it has to exclude most people most of the time. That's not cruelty—it's the nature of meaningful language. Words that include everything describe nothing.

What this looks like: When your child's teacher goes above and beyond, you write a thank-you note praising her dedication and creativity. When a colleague helps you through a difficult project, you acknowledge their generosity and competence. When a friend supports you through grief, you tell them they're a good friend, not a *hero*. None of these people need to be called heroes to feel valued. In fact, they're honored more precisely—and therefore more genuinely—when we name what they actually did.

And finally, we ask ourselves whether we're really honoring someone or just performing gratitude. Real honor names what's actually true about a person. False honor cheapens truth. If you call someone a hero who isn't one, you haven't honored them—you've diminished the standard by which real heroism might be recognized.

What this looks like: Before you post "heroes work here" or "thank you heroes," stop and ask: Am I describing people who voluntarily risked serious harm for others? Or am I describing people who showed up and did their jobs well under difficult circumstances? If it's the latter, find different words—specific, accurate words that honor what they actually did. "Thank you for your dedication during an impossible year" honors a teacher more genuinely than "thank you, hero" because it names the actual virtue she demonstrated.

The soldier who covers a grenade with his own body doesn't need us to expand the definition of heroism to include everyone. The stranger who dives into a river to save a drowning child doesn't need us to make heroism more accessible. The bystander who charges an armed shooter to protect others doesn't need us to democratize the word.

They need us to guard it. To keep it sharp. To make sure that when someone actually does something heroic, we have a word left that can recognize it.

I want to end this chapter on a personal note. I come from a family of military service members. My father was an Air National Guard aircraft mechanic. So was I. My son is a United States Marine. My nephew served in the U.S. Army. My grandfather was an infantryman present at the liberation of the death camps at the end of World War Two. Between us, we span four generations of military service.

And I can tell you this: none of us are heroes for that service alone.

We answered when called. We did our jobs, sometimes under difficult circumstances. We fulfilled our obligations. That deserves respect—the same respect we'd give any person who does their work faithfully. But it's not heroism.

When we call everyone a hero, we dishonor the people who actually were. We tell the young Marine who might face a moment of genuine choice that his choice won't look any different from showing up to formation. We tell the soldier who might have to decide whether to cover that grenade that his decision is no more significant than his buddy's decision to reenlist. That's not generosity. That's theft. We're stealing the language they'll need when the moment comes.

My son doesn't need me to call him a hero. He needs me to guard the word so that if he ever has to be one, the word will still mean something. That's what fathers do. That's what a culture should do. Reserve the word. Keep it sharp. Let most of us be ordinary—faithful, decent, reliable. And when someone steps forward into danger for the sake of another, when someone makes the choice most of us hope we'd make but can't know for certain we would, we'll have a word that recognizes what they've done.

We'll have the word *hero*, and it will mean what it always meant.

Six

BIGOT

The devil...always sends errors into the world in pairs—pairs of opposites. He relies on your extra dislike of one to draw you into the opposite.
—C.S. Lewis

In 2015, a college professor in Indiana made a comment during a lecture on marriage and family. She mentioned, in passing, that traditional religious communities often view marriage as a lifelong covenant between a man and a woman. She wasn't advocating for that view—she was describing it as part of the landscape of American religious belief. Within days, she received emails accusing her of bigotry. Students filed complaints. The word appeared repeatedly in various forms in online forums: *bigot, bigoted, bigotry.*

She hadn't expressed hatred. She hadn't advocated discrimination. She hadn't even stated a personal position. She'd described what millions of Americans believe. But description had become indistinguishable from endorsement, and endorsement had become indistinguishable from hatred.

That's what happened to the word *bigot*—and to its cousins: racism, sexism, homophobia, transphobia, and the ever-expanding suffix family of -ism, -ist, and -phobe.

These words once carried serious moral weight. They named real evils. A bigot was someone who harbored persistent, irrational hatred toward a group of people based on immutable characteristics. Racism described the ideology that some races were inherently superior to others. Sexism meant the belief that one sex was fundamentally less capable or less valuable. These weren't casual terms. They were moral diagnostics—scalpel words used to identify genuine injustice.

But over the past two decades, these words have undergone what might be called linguistic inflation. Like a currency printed too freely, they've lost value through overuse. Today, "bigot" is often deployed not to describe persistent hatred but to shut down disagreement. It's become a rhetorical weapon rather than a diagnostic tool.

The shift happened gradually, in ways that seemed reasonable at each step. If someone advocates for laws that harm a particular group, isn't that a form of bigotry? If someone holds beliefs that cause pain, even unintentionally, doesn't that reveal prejudice? If someone fails to affirm another person's identity, isn't that a kind of violence?

Each question has some logic behind it. But the cumulative effect has been the collapse of any distinction between hatred and disagreement, between prejudice and principle, between malice and mistake. Once those distinctions vanish, the words become useless for their original purpose—because they no longer identify anything specific.

Here's what the inflation looks like in practice.

A business owner says she believes marriage is between a man and a woman, based on her religious convictions. She serves everyone who walks through her door. She hires without regard to personal life. She simply holds a traditional view of marriage. That view is now widely labeled homophobic. Not just wrong—hateful. The word that once described people who beat gay men to death now applies to someone who holds a millennia-old religious belief.

A parent says he's uncomfortable with his seven-year-old being taught about gender identity in school. He's not advocating harm. He's not expressing hatred toward anyone. He's simply questioning whether the topic is age-appropriate. He's called transphobic. The conversation ends. The label removes any need to engage with his actual concern.

A scholar publishes research suggesting that some observed differences between men and women may have biological components. She's careful, nuanced, aware of the complexity. She acknowledges cultural factors. But the research is deemed sexist. Colleagues distance themselves. Outlets refuse to publish her follow-up work. The label becomes a professional death sentence, regardless of the evidence.

A person says "I don't see color—I just see people." They mean it as an expression of equality, an attempt to say that race doesn't determine worth. But they're told this statement itself is racist. Colorblindness, they're informed, is a form of erasure. The very attempt to transcend racial categories becomes evidence of prejudice.

This same collapse—the inability to distinguish depiction from endorsement—shows up in how we've treated classic literature.. Mark Twain's *Adventures of Huckleberry Finn*—written explicitly as an anti-slavery novel, structured to show a boy overcoming the racist conditioning of his society—has been removed from some schools' curricula because it contains the racial slur that characters in 1840s Missouri would have used. The slur appears because Twain was depicting the world as it was, not as it should be, showing how Huck gradually learned to see Jim's full humanity despite the dehumanizing language around him. That's the moral architecture of the entire novel.

But if we can't distinguish between a book that uses racist language to condemn racism and a book that uses racist language to endorse it, we've lost a crucial intellectual tool. The label *racist* gets applied to the book itself, and the conversation ends. We don't teach the difficult context. We don't help students think about how language functions differently in different historical moments, or how an author can depict evil without endorsing it. We just remove the book and call it progress.

To Kill a Mockingbird has faced the same treatment—a novel explicitly about combating racism in the Jim Crow South, removed because it contains language authentic to that setting, spoken by characters the novel itself condemns.

I recently bought a copy of *Little Black Sambo* for one of our grandchildren. The book itself isn't racist—it's an 1899 story by a Scottish woman about a clever Indian boy who outsmarts tigers. But the name "Sambo" became associated with

American racial caricatures that had nothing to do with the original text. Rather than teach children that distinction—how words accumulate meanings, how context matters, how we can engage thoughtfully with cultural artifacts from different eras—we disappeared the book entirely. It's easier to call it racist than to think carefully about what racism actually means.

Do not misunderstand me: **None of this excuses actual racism in literature**. Books that promote racial hierarchy, that dehumanize people, that argue for discrimination all deserve criticism and contextualization. But there's a difference between *Uncle Tom's Cabin* and *The Turner Diaries*, between *Huckleberry Finn* and a minstrel show. When we lose the ability to make those distinctions, when "racist" or "bigot" becomes a label we apply to anything that makes us uncomfortable, we're not protecting anyone. We're just ensuring that the next generation won't understand how racism actually worked, how it was challenged, or how to think critically about the relationship between language and harm.

The cruel irony is that by labeling these anti-racist books as racist, we lose some of the most powerful tools for teaching *about* racism. Students who never read *Huckleberry Finn* don't learn how casual dehumanization operates in daily language, or how moral growth requires questioning the assumptions you were raised with. They get a sanitized curriculum where no one ever says anything offensive, which means they never develop the critical thinking skills to recognize and resist racism when they encounter it in the real world

In all of these cases, the moral charge is catastrophic. To be called a bigot, a racist, a homophobe—or any one of a myriad of other -ists, -isms, or -phobes—is to be cast out of decent society. Jobs are lost. Reputations are destroyed. Relationships end. The label doesn't invite conversation—it ends it. And because the consequences are so severe, the words have become tools of power rather than tools of clarity.

This isn't to say that real bigotry doesn't exist. It does. Hatred based on race, sex, sexual orientation, and identity is real, persistent, and destructive. People still face genuine discrimination. Prejudice still operates in hiring, housing, law enforcement, and daily life. The problem isn't that we're calling out too much injustice. The problem is that we're using the same words for actual hatred and for ordinary disagreement—and in doing so, we've made it nearly impossible to distinguish between them.

When everything is bigotry, nothing is. C.S. Lewis understood this pattern. The devil, he said, sends errors in pairs—pairs of opposites. One error is to deny that bigotry exists at all, to wave away complaints as oversensitivity, to refuse to see injustice even when it's obvious. The opposite error is to see bigotry everywhere, to interpret every disagreement as hatred, to treat every discomfort as evidence of moral failure.

Both errors are dangerous. The first allows real evil to flourish unchecked. The second destroys the possibility of honest conversation and makes enemies of people who might otherwise be persuaded. Lewis was warning against both extremes. But our moment seems especially vulnerable to the second.

The inflation of these words creates several problems that compound over time.

First, it produces false positives at scale. When the bar for *"bigotry"* drops low enough, enormous numbers of people get swept into the category who don't belong there. A grandmother who struggles with new pronouns isn't a bigot—she's adjusting to linguistic changes that arrived faster than her capacity to adapt. A person who believes in biological sex categories isn't a transphobe—they're holding a view that was uncontroversial until very recently. A person who questions a policy isn't necessarily motivated by hatred—they might just disagree about means, not ends.

These false positives do harm in both directions. They wound people who are accused unjustly, and they create cynicism that damages the ability to respond to real bigotry when it appears. If you're called a racist for holding a view that half the country shares, you stop trusting the people doing the labeling. And when actual racism appears, the word has lost its power to alert you.

Second, the inflation creates perverse incentives. If *bigot* becomes a word you can deploy to win arguments, people will deploy it. If calling someone *homophobic* ends a debate in your favor, the temptation is to use the label even when it doesn't apply. The word becomes strategy rather than description. And once that happens, the moral vocabulary of a culture becomes corrupted—words no longer reveal truth; they serve power.

Third, it prevents people from growing. If someone holds a view rooted in ignorance rather than malice, the appropriate response is education, not excommunication. But if we treat every mistaken belief as though it were hatred, we remove any incentive for the person to reconsider. Why listen to someone who's just called you a bigot? Why engage with people who've labeled you evil? The conversation ends, and the person hardens in their position—not because they're incapable of change, but because change requires trust, and trust has been destroyed.

Fourth, it protects actual bigots. When the word is used indiscriminately, real bigots can point to the overuse and say, "*See?* They call everyone a bigot. The word means nothing." And they're partly right. The boy who cried wolf didn't make wolves less dangerous—he made people stop believing in warnings. Linguistic inflation does the same thing. The more we cheapen these words, the harder it becomes to sound the alarm when real danger appears.

Fifth, and perhaps most tragically, the inflation harms the very people these words were meant to protect. When someone experiences actual discrimination—when they're denied a job because of their race, when they're harassed because of their identity, when they face genuine hatred—they need language strong enough to name what's happened. But if the same words have already been used to describe someone's grandma who used the wrong pronoun, the words no longer carry weight. Victims of real injustice find themselves using a vocabulary that's been devalued by overuse.

The question, then, is how we restore precision.

First, we must recover the distinction between disagreement and hatred or fear. People can hold views you find wrong, even deeply wrong, without being motivated by malice. A person who believes marriage should be between a man and a woman may not align with your view on the issue, but that belief alone doesn't make them a bigot. Bigotry requires not just a position but a posture—persistent, irrational animosity. If the person treats everyone with dignity, serves everyone equally, and simply holds a traditional belief, they're not a bigot. They're someone you disagree with.

This doesn't mean all views are equally valid. Some beliefs are better than others. Some positions cause more harm than others. But we have other words for *wrong* and *harmful*. We don't need to use *bigot* unless we mean a harmful, persistent hatred.

Second, we have to stop treating discomfort as evidence of bigotry. The fact that someone's view makes you uncomfortable doesn't prove the view is rooted in hatred. Discomfort might mean the view challenges your assumptions. It might mean you're encountering a perspective you haven't considered. It might mean the conversation is difficult—but difficult conversations aren't inherently violent.

Third, we must allow room for ignorance, confusion, and mistakes. Not everyone who says the wrong thing is a bigot. Some people are simply uninformed. Some are navigating rapid cultural changes and stumbling as they go. Some are trying to be respectful but lack the vocabulary. If we treat every misstep as moral failure, we eliminate the possibility of growth. Grace doesn't mean ignoring harm—it means distinguishing between harm caused by malice and harm caused by ignorance.

Fourth, we must resist the temptation to use these words strategically. If you call someone a bigot because it's effective rather than because it's accurate, you're not fighting injustice—you're weaponizing language. And once language becomes a weapon, trust collapses. People stop listening to each other. They stop believing each other. They retreat into tribes where everyone already agrees, and the possibility of persuasion disappears.

Fifth, we must accept that not every claim of bigotry is valid. This is uncomfortable, because it requires us to judge—to say, in some cases, "No, that's not bigotry. That's disagreement." It requires us to tolerate the possibility that someone who feels harmed may be misinterpreting the situation. Feelings are real, but they're not always accurate. A person can feel attacked without being attacked. They can feel unsafe without being in danger. And if we automatically validate every claim without scrutiny, we lose the ability to distinguish real harm from perceived harm.

This is difficult work, because it requires nuance in a moment that rewards certainty. It requires patience in a culture that demands immediate judgment. It requires the humility to admit that we might be wrong—that what we've labeled bigotry might actually be something else.

But the alternative is worse. If we continue inflating these words, we'll eventually lose them entirely. They'll become noise—labels people ignore because they've been overused to the point of meaninglessness. And when that happens, we'll have no vocabulary left to name real hatred when it appears.

Real bigotry still exists. People are still harassed, excluded, and harmed because of their identity. Racism still operates in hiring, policing, and housing. Hatred still motivates violence. These realities demand language strong enough to name them. But that language only works if we guard it—if we use it precisely, sparingly, and honestly.

The words bigot, racist, sexist, homophobe, and transphobe were given to us to name genuine evil. They're too important to waste on disagreements. They're too powerful to use casually. And they're too necessary to let them become meaningless through inflation.

If we want these words to retain their power—if we want them to be available when real injustice appears, we have to stop using them as weapons and start using them as scalpels again.

Precision isn't cruelty. It's care. It's the recognition that language matters, that truth matters, and that the people these words were meant to protect deserve vocabulary that can still distinguish between those who hate them and those who simply see the world differently.

We owe them that much. And we owe ourselves the possibility of living in a society where words still mean something, where conversation is still possible, and where moral language hasn't been devalued into irrelevance.

The recovery of these words begins the moment we stop using them carelessly—when we pause before labeling someone, when we ask whether the charge is accurate, when we choose a less catastrophic word if a less catastrophic word is true. It begins when we remember that the boy who cried wolf didn't just lose credibility. He got people killed. And it begins when we decide that protecting these words matters more than winning arguments.

Because in the end, we're going to need them. Real bigotry hasn't disappeared. Real hatred still does real harm. And when it shows up—when it needs to be named clearly, called out sharply, and opposed firmly—we're going to need language that hasn't been hollowed out by overuse. We're going to need words that still carry weight. And if we've spent them all on arguments that didn't require them, they won't be there when we need them most.

SEVEN

GRATITUDE

It is not happiness that makes us grateful, but gratefulness that makes us happy.
—David Steindl-Rast

The first six chapters have looked outward—at the words we've broken in public, the language we've weaponized in argument, the vocabulary we've hollowed out in discourse. But the thinning doesn't stop at the border between public and private life. It follows us home. The chapters that follow look inward—at the words that shape how we live with ourselves and with the people we love. The damage is harder to measure there, and so is the recovery. But it may matter more.

Go around the table at any Thanksgiving dinner in America and you'll hear the same ritual. Each person says what they're grateful for. The answers come quickly, almost reflexively: "I'm grateful for my health." "I'm grateful for this time together." "I'm grateful for my job." "I'm blessed."

The words are sincere—or at least, they're not insincere. But they're also generic, almost placeholders. Rarely does anyone name a specific person who helped them. Rarely does anyone mention a particular kindness received. Rarely does anyone articulate what, exactly, they're grateful for—just the vague category of things they're supposed to appreciate. Gratitude has become a ritual we perform rather than a reality we inhabit. Gratitude has become a mood we are supposed to feel rather than a posture we are meant to live. It has become something you express on Thanksgiving or write in a journal as part of a wellness routine, but it has lost its older, deeper function: the recognition that your life is sustained by gifts you didn't earn and cannot repay.

Gratitude used to mean something more specific than general appreciation. It wasn't just a warm feeling you summoned when things were going well. It was a moral orientation—a way of seeing the world that acknowledged dependence, honored givers, and resisted the illusion of self-sufficiency.

The word itself comes from Latin *gratia*, meaning grace or favor—something freely given, unearned. To be grateful was to recognize that much of what you had came not from your own effort but from the generosity, sacrifice, or simple presence of others. It required humility. It required attention. And it required a certain discipline, the willingness to notice what had been given before noticing what had been withheld.

That understanding has eroded. Gratitude has been reduced to something like an emotional vitamin—a practice you're told is good for mental health, a technique for cultivating positivity, a strategy for feeling better about your life. It's been instrumentalized. Gratitude journals promise to boost your mood. Gratitude exercises promise to reduce anxiety. Gratitude is now something you do for yourself rather than something you owe to others.

The shift is subtle but consequential. When gratitude becomes self-focused, it stops being gratitude. It becomes a form of self-care disguised as virtue. You're not actually thanking anyone—you're managing your emotions. You're not recognizing dependence—you're practicing a technique. And the result is that the moral structure of gratitude collapses. What was once a relational virtue—something that bound people together through acknowledgment and reciprocity—becomes a private feeling that doesn't require anyone else at all.

This wouldn't matter much if gratitude were a minor virtue, something decorative you could take or leave. But it's not. Gratitude is foundational. It's one of the earliest moral recognitions a child can make: *I need others. Others give to me. I should respond.* That recognition is the beginning of relationship, the beginning of obligation, the beginning of community. Without gratitude, human life becomes a zero-sum game of acquisition and complaint. With gratitude, life becomes an exchange of gifts—imperfect, unequal, but binding, nonetheless.

The loss of gratitude shows up everywhere, but especially in the way people talk about what they have.

Entitlement has become the default posture. People speak of their rights, their needs, their expectations—but rarely of their debts. The language of "I deserve" has crowded out the language of "I received." Even when people acknowledge good fortune, they often frame it in passive terms: "I'm blessed" rather than "Someone blessed me." The grammar itself erases the giver.

This shows up most clearly in how we talk about success. When successful people tell their stories, they emphasize their own hard work, determination, and talent. They mention obstacles they overcame, sacrifices they made, risks they took. All of this is true. But it's not the whole truth. What they often leave out is the part that gratitude would require them to acknowledge: the advantages they started with, the help they received, the breaks they caught, the people who gave them opportunities they hadn't earned yet.

This isn't to diminish genuine achievement. Hard work matters. Talent matters. Determination matters. But they matter within a context that includes gift, grace, and unearned advantage. The person who works hard and succeeds had parents who taught them the value of hard work. They had teachers who recognized their potential. They had a society stable enough that hard work could pay off. They had health and circumstances that allowed them to work hard in the first place. None of this diminishes their achievement. But all of it calls for gratitude.

This isn't just about manners. It's about perception. A person who lives without gratitude begins to see the world as though it owes them something—as though their comfort, their success, their happiness were entitlements that should arrive automatically. When reality fails to meet those expectations, the response is resentment. And resentment is the opposite of gratitude. Where gratitude enlarges the soul, resentment shrinks it. Where gratitude creates generosity, resentment breeds bitterness.

David Steindl-Rast's line captures something essential. Gratitude isn't a response to good circumstances; it's a way of interpreting circumstances that makes happiness possible even when circumstances are difficult. A grateful person can endure hardship because they see the good that remains. An ungrateful person can have abundance and still feel deprived because they see only what's missing.

This is why gratitude was once considered a discipline rather than a feeling. You didn't wait to feel grateful before expressing it. You practiced gratitude as an act of will, as a way of training the heart to notice gifts rather than grievances. You thanked people not because you were overcome with emotion but because you recognized a debt. You expressed gratitude even when it felt awkward, even when the gift was imperfect, even when you'd rather not acknowledge dependence.

That discipline has largely disappeared. We've replaced it with the idea that gratitude should be spontaneous, authentic, heartfelt—and if it's not, we don't bother. But spontaneous gratitude is rare. Most of the time, gratitude has to be chosen. It has to be practiced against the grain of a mind that's inclined to notice problems rather than blessings, to focus on what's wrong rather than what's right.

The result is a culture that is increasingly fluent in complaint and increasingly inarticulate in thanks.

Think about how people talk online. Social media has become a vast engine of grievance. People catalog injustices, voice frustrations, document disappointments. That's not entirely bad—sometimes complaints are justified and voicing them is necessary. But the ratio is wildly skewed. For every post expressing gratitude, there are dozens expressing dissatisfaction. And over time, that ratio shapes how people see the world. The mind becomes practiced at noticing what's wrong and unpracticed at noticing what's right.

Or think about how people talk about their jobs. Complaints about work are socially acceptable, almost expected. Expressing gratitude for your job—even if it's a good job, even if you're well-paid, even if you're doing meaningful work—can sound naïve or out of touch. The default assumption is that work is something you endure, not something you might be grateful for. And while some jobs genuinely are exploitative or soul-crushing, many aren't. But the cultural script makes it hard to acknowledge that without sounding like you're bragging or bootlicking.

Or consider how people talk about their families. It's become common to joke about how annoying your spouse is, how exhausting your kids are, how difficult your parents are. Some of that is just humor—a way of coping with stress. But it's also revealing. The things people complain about publicly are often the things they take for granted privately. A person who jokes endlessly about their spouse's flaws may not realize how rarely they express gratitude for their spouse's presence. A person who vents about parenting may forget to articulate the depth of love they feel for their children.

None of this is malicious. It's just habit. And habits shape perception. If you practice complaint more than gratitude, complaint becomes your default lens. You start seeing the world as a place that disappoints you rather than sustains you. And once that happens, even genuine blessings start to feel insufficient.

The antidote isn't forced positivity or toxic optimism. It's not pretending everything is fine when it isn't. It's not suppressing legitimate grievances or ignoring real problems. The antidote is simply remembering that gratitude and honesty can coexist. You can acknowledge difficulty and recognize gift. You can name what's broken and honor what's intact. You can complain when complaint is warranted and give thanks when thanks are due.

But that requires intention. It requires the discipline to notice. And it requires recovering the grammar of gratitude—the ability to see, name, and respond to what's been given.

The grammar of gratitude has four movements, and most of us stop after the first or second.

First: Perception. You have to notice the gift. This sounds simple, but it's not. Most of what sustains your life is invisible to you because it's constant. The people who love you. The systems that work. The efforts others make on your behalf. These things disappear into the background unless you deliberately attend to them. Perception is the discipline of noticing what would be missed if it were gone.

Second: Recognition. Once you notice the gift, you have to acknowledge what it costs. Someone gave time, effort, money, patience, skill. Something was sacrificed —however small —so that you could receive. Recognition means seeing the giver, not just the gift. It means understanding that what you have didn't materialize out of nowhere. It came from somewhere. It came from someone.

Third: Articulation. Gratitude that remains internal is incomplete. It has to be spoken. Not because the other person needs to hear it (though they often do), but because speaking it changes you. Articulating gratitude makes it real in a way that feeling it does not. It moves gratitude from the realm of private sentiment into the realm of relationship. And it trains your mind to name goodness when you see it.

Fourth: Response. Gratitude that doesn't produce action isn't gratitude—it's sentimentality. True gratitude creates obligation. Not the heavy, oppressive kind of obligation, but the kind that binds people together. When you recognize that someone has given to you, you naturally want to give in return—if not to them, then to someone else. Gratitude makes you generous. It opens the hand that was inclined to close.

Most modern gratitude stops at the first movement if it gets there at all. We notice, vaguely, that things are okay. We feel, vaguely, that we should be thankful. But we don't name the givers. We don't articulate the gift. We don't respond with reciprocity. And so, gratitude remains thin—a fleeting feeling rather than a shaping force.

Recovering gratitude means recovering all four movements. It means training yourself to notice what you've been given, to recognize who gave it, to name it aloud, and to let it change how you live. It also means recovering gratitude in relationships where it's become rare.

One of the quiet tragedies of modern life is how seldom people express gratitude to the people closest to them. Spouses take each other for granted. Parents assume their children know they're appreciated. Friends assume affection is understood without being spoken. And over time, relationships grow brittle—not because love has died, but because the expressions of love have stopped.

Gratitude is one of the simplest and most powerful ways to keep relationships alive. A sentence—sincere, specific, unprompted—can do more to strengthen a marriage than hours of conversation. "Thank you for making dinner every night this week." "I'm grateful you listened when I was upset." "I don't say it enough, but I notice what you do." These aren't grand gestures. They're small acknowledgments. But they matter. They signal that the other person is seen, that their efforts aren't invisible, that their presence isn't taken for granted.

The same is true for friendships. People drift apart not because of conflict but because of silence. One person assumes the other knows they're valued. The other person, not hearing it, begins to wonder if the relationship still matters. A single expression of gratitude—"I'm really glad we stayed in touch" or "That conversation last month helped more than you know"—can re-anchor a friendship that was starting to float away.

Even professional relationships benefit from gratitude. A manager who thanks employees specifically and sincerely creates loyalty that no salary can buy. A colleague who acknowledges help rather than taking it for granted builds trust. Gratitude in the workplace isn't soft or sentimental—it's strategic. It strengthens the bonds that allow people to work together under pressure.

But all of this requires overcoming the awkwardness of sincerity. We live in an ironic age, one that's uncomfortable with earnestness. Expressing gratitude can feel vulnerable. It exposes you. It admits dependence. It risks sounding corny. And so people hold back. They assume the other person knows. They tell themselves it doesn't need to be said. But it does. It always does.

Gratitude also requires humility—the recognition that you are not self-made, that your life is threaded through with debts you can never fully repay. This runs against the modern myth of the self-sufficient individual who owes nothing to anyone. But that myth is a lie. Every single person alive depends on others—for survival, for comfort, for meaning. The food you ate today was grown, harvested, transported, and prepared by people you'll never meet. The roads you drove on were built by workers whose names you don't know. The language you speak was handed to you by ancestors who've been dead for centuries. You didn't earn any of this. You inherited it. You received it. And the appropriate response is gratitude.

That recognition doesn't diminish you. It grounds you. It reminds you that you're part of something larger than yourself—a web of relationships, obligations, and gifts that stretches backward through time and forward into the future. Gratitude is what keeps that web intact.

Finally, gratitude has to be taught. It doesn't develop automatically. Children are naturally egocentric. Babies are innately selfish. They assume the world revolves around them and their needs. Gratitude is the slow realization that other people exist, that other people give, and that those gifts deserve acknowledgment. Teaching a child to say "thank you" is teaching them to see beyond themselves. It's moral formation disguised as manners.

But teaching gratitude isn't just about enforcing politeness. It's about helping children notice the structure of their lives—the countless small acts of care that sustain them. "Who made this meal?" "Who drove you to practice?" "Who fixed your bike?" These questions train attention. They make visible what was invisible. And over time, they shape a person who sees the world as full of gifts rather than entitlements.

Adults need this training too. We drift into ingratitude not because we're bad people but because we stop paying attention. Recovering gratitude means relearning how to notice—how to see what we've been given, who gave it, and what it cost. And it means practicing the discipline of saying so.

Gratitude won't fix everything. It won't erase injustice or solve systemic problems or make hardship disappear. But it will change how you carry those things. It will give you resilience in difficulty, generosity in abundance, and perspective in confusion. It will make you easier to live with, easier to work with, and easier to love.

And in a culture starved for sincerity, it will make you a small, quiet source of grace—the kind of person others are grateful to know.

Gratitude is not a feeling. It's a practice. It's a posture. It's a way of seeing. And it begins the moment you decide to notice what you've been given and say so.

EIGHT

RESPONSIBILITY

The price of greatness is responsibility.
—Winston Churchill

The word *responsibility* has become heavy in a way it wasn't meant to be. Somewhere along the line, it stopped sounding like dignity and started sounding like drudgery. When people hear "responsibility," they really hear "obligation, burden, constraint"—something imposed from the outside that limits freedom and demands sacrifice. The modern ear hears "responsibility" and thinks: "something I have to do that I'd rather not."

But responsibility used to mean something different. It meant answerability—the condition of being someone whose word could be trusted, whose commitments could be counted on, whose presence made things more stable rather than less. It was the mark of adulthood, the sign that a person had moved from dependence to agency. Responsibility wasn't what limited you. It was what made you real.

The shift happened gradually, part of a larger cultural move toward viewing freedom as the absence of constraint rather than the presence of purpose. If freedom means doing whatever you want whenever you want, then responsibility becomes its opposite—an enemy to be minimized or avoided. But that's a thin understanding of freedom. Freedom without responsibility isn't liberation; it's adolescence extended indefinitely. And adolescence, however appealing in the moment, is an exhausting way to live.

Here's what responsibility actually is. It's the recognition that your choices have consequences, that those consequences affect others, and that you are accountable for the effects you create. It's the willingness to be answerable—not in the legal sense of avoiding punishment, but in the moral sense of owning what you've done and making it right when you've done wrong.

Responsibility gives shape to a life. Without it, days drift. Commitments dissolve. Relationships fray. A person without responsibility isn't free—they're unmoored, blown by impulse and circumstance, unable to build anything that lasts. With responsibility, a life gains coherence. It has direction. It has meaning. People know what to expect from you because you've made yourself predictable in the best sense—reliable, steady, present.

The resistance to responsibility comes partly from how it's often framed: as a burden imposed by society, parents, employers, or tradition. "You have to get a job." "You have to settle down." "You have to grow up." When responsibility is presented as obligation without purpose, it feels oppressive. And people resist oppression, even when the resistance harms them.

But responsibility isn't oppression. It's not something forced on you by external authorities demanding compliance. It's something you claim for yourself because you recognize that being a person—a full, adult person—requires it. You don't take responsibility because someone makes you. You take it because the alternative is remaining a child forever, dependent on others to manage what you won't manage yourself.

The clearest sign of responsibility is what you do when no one is watching. A responsible person keeps promises even when breaking them would be easier. They show up even when showing up is inconvenient. They tell the truth even when lying would spare them discomfort. They clean up their own messes even when no one would notice if they didn't. Responsibility is what you do in the unseen moments when character is the only enforcement mechanism.

The opposite of responsibility isn't freedom—it's evasion. And evasion always extracts a cost.

When people evade responsibility, someone else absorbs it. A parent who won't discipline their child forces teachers to manage the chaos. An employee who won't own their mistakes forces coworkers to cover for them. A citizen who won't engage with difficult problems forces others to carry the load. Evasion doesn't eliminate responsibility; it redistributes it—usually to people who are already carrying more than their share.

This is why responsibility has a moral dimension. It's not just about personal success or individual flourishing. It's about fairness. It's about recognizing that you live in a web of relationships and obligations, and that your refusal to carry your part of the load means someone else has to carry it for you. Every time you dodge responsibility, you're imposing on someone else—often invisibly, often on people who can't afford the extra weight.

Modern culture has developed an entire vocabulary for evading responsibility. We talk about being "triggered" as though external events control our reactions. We describe ourselves as "victims of circumstance" as though circumstances eliminate agency. We frame every struggle as systemic oppression as though systems are the only forces that matter. Some of this language names real phenomena—trauma is real, circumstances do constrain, systems do oppress. But the language has been overextended to the point where it now functions as an all-purpose escape hatch. If everything is someone else's fault, nothing is yours.

Fault is about what caused a problem. Responsibility is about who's going to solve it. They sometimes overlap, but not always. You can be responsible for fixing something you didn't break. You can be responsible for dealing with consequences you didn't cause.

Consider a straightforward example: a driver runs a red light and totals your car. Fault is clear—they caused the accident. But you're still responsible for what happens next. You have to file the insurance claim, arrange the rental car, deal with repairs or replacement, handle the medical appointments if you're injured. None of that is your fault. All of it is your responsibility.

Or consider something more complex: a person grows up in a chaotic home with parents who never taught basic life skills. It's not their fault they weren't taught how to manage money, maintain relationships, or handle conflict constructively. But it is their responsibility to learn these things as an adult. The person who spends their life blaming their parents for what they didn't receive never develops what they need. The person who says "my parents failed me, and now I have to learn what I should have been taught" is taking responsibility without denying fault. They're not pretending they caused the problem—they're accepting that they're the only one who can solve it.

This distinction matters because conflating fault and responsibility creates two opposite failures. Some people refuse all responsibility by claiming they're not at fault: "I didn't cause this problem, so it's not my job to fix it." They're technically right about causation, but they're still living in the wreckage, waiting for someone else to clean it up. Other people accept fault for things that aren't their fault, loading themselves with false guilt: "Everything bad in my life is my fault." This produces paralysis—they're so busy punishing themselves they never actually fix anything.

The mature position is different: "*I*'m responsible for my response, regardless of who caused the situation." This isn't fair in some cosmic sense—it would be more fair if the person who caused the problem had to fix it. But fairness isn't the point. Agency is. The moment you accept responsibility for dealing with what's in front of you, you regain power. You stop being a victim of circumstances and become someone capable of responding to them.

The person who understands this distinction can say both things at once: "This isn't my fault" and "This is my responsibility." That's not a contradiction. That's maturity.

The cost of this evasion is devastating, especially for the person doing the evading. A person who refuses responsibility for their life never develops competence. They never learn that they can influence outcomes, that effort matters, that discipline produces results. They remain perpetually dependent—not on parents or institutions, but on the belief that someone else is supposed to fix things for them. And when no one does, they grow resentful, convinced the world has failed them, blind to the ways they've failed themselves.

Responsibility isn't glamorous. It doesn't announce itself. It doesn't get celebrated on social media. Most of the work of responsibility happens in mundane, unglamorous ways: paying bills on time, showing up when you said you would, following through even when the initial excitement has worn off, repairing relationships instead of abandoning them, admitting fault instead of deflecting blame.

But these small acts of responsibility compound. Over time, they build trust. They create stability. They make you someone others can rely on. And that reliability—being someone who can be counted on—is one of the highest forms of dignity available to a human being.

The digital age has made evading responsibility easier than ever. You can ghost someone instead of having a difficult conversation. You can delete a post instead of standing by what you said. You can block critics instead of responding to legitimate questions. You can curate an image of responsibility—posting about causes, signaling virtue, performing concern—without actually doing anything that costs you something. The appearance of responsibility has never been easier to manufacture. Actual responsibility has never been easier to avoid.

But the digital trail doesn't lie, even when we think it does. The person who ghosts repeatedly earns a reputation for unreliability. The person who deletes and deflects earns a reputation for cowardice. The person who performs without producing earns a reputation for hollowness. These reputations accumulate invisibly until they become unavoidable. And then people wonder why no one trusts them, why opportunities don't come, why relationships don't last. They've spent years avoiding responsibility while thinking they were getting away with it. But they weren't. They were just deferring the cost.

Churchill's line about responsibility being the price of greatness captures something essential. Greatness isn't talent or intelligence or charisma. Those are gifts, and gifts alone don't produce anything meaningful. Greatness is what happens when someone with gifts accepts responsibility for using them well. It's the teacher who doesn't just show up but prepares. It's the parent who doesn't just provide but guides. It's the leader who doesn't just occupy a position but serves the people in their care.

Responsibility also has a liberating dimension that's often overlooked. When you accept responsibility for your life, you gain agency. You stop being a passive recipient of whatever happens to you and become an active participant in shaping outcomes. This doesn't mean you control everything—no one does. But it means you control more than you thought. The person who takes responsibility for their health makes different choices than the person who blames genetics. The person who takes responsibility for their relationships repairs rather than abandons. The person who takes responsibility for their career develops skills rather than nursing grievances.

Agency isn't the same as control, but it's related. Agency is the recognition that your choices matter, that you have some influence over what happens next, that you're not simply a leaf blown by the wind. And that recognition—"I can affect this"—is one of the most stabilizing realizations a person can have.

The recovery of responsibility begins with language. We have to stop using words that erase agency and start using words that restore it. Instead of "I can't," try "I haven't yet figured out how." Instead of "They made me feel," try "I felt when they did that." Instead of "It's not my fault," try "What part of this can I influence?"

This isn't about self-blame or denying real constraints. It's about recovering the distinction between what you can control and what you can't—and then focusing your energy on the part you can actually affect. Responsibility doesn't mean pretending you caused everything. It means accepting accountability for your response to whatever happens.

It also means recovering the idea that responsibility can be chosen, not just assigned. The most meaningful responsibilities are often the ones we volunteer for—the ones we step into because we see a need and decide to meet it. The parent who stays. The neighbor who helps. The coworker who takes the lead on a difficult project. The citizen who engages instead of complaining from the sidelines. These are people who didn't wait to be told what their responsibility was. They saw what needed doing and did it.

That kind of responsibility is the opposite of burden. It's purpose. It's meaning. It's the recognition that you can make a difference, however small, and that making that difference is worth the cost.

Recovering responsibility also means teaching it. Children don't naturally develop it—they have to be guided into it. This happens through small, age-appropriate steps: making their bed, feeding the dog, finishing homework, keeping commitments to friends. Each of these teaches the same lesson: your actions matter, other people depend on you, and following through is how you earn trust.

But teaching responsibility has become difficult in a culture that prioritizes children's immediate happiness over their long-term character. Parents who shield children from consequences—redoing homework the child didn't complete, making excuses when the child fails to show up, intervening in every conflict—aren't protecting their children. They're preventing them from developing the capacity to handle difficulty. And children who never develop that capacity become adults who can't function without constant intervention.

Teaching responsibility happens in stages, each appropriate to the child's age and capacity. A five-year-old can be responsible for putting their toys away before bed. A ten-year-old can be responsible for their homework, their backpack, and feeding the family pet. A fifteen-year-old can be responsible for a part-time job, managing their own schedule, and maintaining relationships with friends. Each stage builds on the previous one, developing the internal mechanism that says, "This is mine to manage."

The key is letting natural consequences teach the lesson. The five-year-old who doesn't put toys away loses the privilege of taking them out the next day. The ten-year-old who forgets their lunch learns what hunger feels like—and remembers their lunch the next day. The fifteen-year-old who shows up late to work gets a warning from their boss, not a rescue from their parents. These consequences aren't cruelty—they're information. They teach cause and effect. They show the child that their choices matter.

But modern parenting has largely abandoned natural consequences in favor of artificial protection. The parent who brings the forgotten lunch to school, who completes the child's science project the night before it's due, who calls the coach to demand their child get more playing time—these parents think they're helping. They're not. They're teaching learned helplessness. They're teaching that someone will always step in, that effort is optional, that consequences can be negotiated away.

The irony is that these parents often justify their intervention with responsibility language: "I'm being a responsible parent by making sure my child succeeds." But responsibility can't be given—it can only be claimed. And a child who never faces the consequences of irresponsibility never learns to be responsible. They learn something else entirely: that other people exist to solve their problems.

This produces adults who can't function independently. The college student who calls their parents to resolve conflicts with roommates. The young employee who expects their boss to manage their emotional state. The adult child who returns home at thirty because they never learned to manage money, keep commitments, or navigate difficulty without rescue. These aren't moral failures—they're training failures. No one taught them that they were capable of handling hard things, so they never developed the capacity.

Teaching responsibility also means resisting the urge to smooth every rough edge out of your child's life. The child who experiences boredom learns to entertain themselves. The child who experiences conflict with friends learns to repair relationships. The child who experiences failure learns to try again differently. The child who experiences disappointment learns that not everything goes their way and they can survive it anyway.

None of this means abandoning children to figure everything out alone. It means scaffolding—providing support while gradually transferring ownership. You don't throw a six-year-old into the deep end of the pool and call it swimming lessons. But you also don't keep them in floaties until they're sixteen. You teach them to swim by being present while they practice, by letting them struggle a little, by letting them go under once or twice so they learn they can get back up.

The parent who teaches responsibility isn't the one who prevents all failure—it's the one who's present for the failure, who helps the child process what went wrong, and who expects them to try again with what they've learned. That's harder than rescuing. It requires watching your child struggle without intervening. It requires believing they're capable even when they're convinced they're not. But it produces adults who can stand on their own, who can be counted on, who understand that their choices create their lives.

Consider the earlier example of what happens when a child forgets their homework. The responsible parent doesn't rush to school with the forgotten assignment—they let the child face the natural consequence of a lower grade or a conversation with the teacher. This feels harsh in the moment. The child is upset. The parent could fix it easily. But fixing it teaches the wrong lesson. It teaches that someone will always rescue you, that your choices don't have real consequences, that responsibility is optional. The child who learns this doesn't develop the internal mechanism that says, "I need to remember my homework because no one else will do it for me." They develop a different mechanism: "Someone will catch me if I fall, so I don't need to watch my step." That might work in childhood. It fails catastrophically in adulthood.

Responsibility is also relational. You don't just take responsibility for yourself—you take it for the people in your care and the communities you belong to. A responsible spouse doesn't just avoid causing harm; they actively work to strengthen the marriage. A responsible parent doesn't just provide food and shelter; they shape character. A responsible citizen doesn't just obey laws; they contribute to the common good.

This is where responsibility becomes stewardship—the recognition that much of what you have isn't really yours. It's been entrusted to you. Your talents, your resources, your influence, your time—all of these are gifts you're meant to use well, not hoard or waste.

Stewardship gets covered in much more detail in Chapter 15, but for now here is how it ties directly to responsibility. Stewardship asks a different question than ownership. Ownership asks: "What can I get from this?" Stewardship asks: "What has this been given to me for?" The talented musician isn't just lucky—they're responsible for what they do with that talent. The person with wealth isn't just successful—they're responsible for whether that wealth serves purposes beyond their own comfort. The person with influence isn't just popular—they're responsible for what they do with the attention they've been given.

This doesn't mean you can't enjoy what you have. It means recognizing that having something creates an obligation to use it well. The opposite of stewardship is waste—the squandering of gifts through neglect, selfishness, or cowardice. And waste, in the end, is a kind of theft. You've taken something that could have served others and used it only to serve yourself. Or worse, you've taken something valuable and let it rot unused.

There's a quiet dignity in living responsibly. The responsible person doesn't need constant validation because their sense of worth comes from within. They know they've kept their promises. They know they've done what they said they'd do. They know that when things went wrong, they owned their part and worked to make it right. That kind of integrity creates a peace that external approval can never provide.

But responsibility requires one more thing: the willingness to fail. Because you will fail. You'll break promises you meant to keep. You'll miss obligations you intended to meet. You'll cause harm you didn't mean to cause. Responsibility doesn't mean perfection—it means accountability. And accountability means admitting when you've failed, apologizing sincerely, and working to repair the damage.

This is why responsibility, truth, and humility go together. The person who can't admit fault can never be truly responsible because they can never be accountable. They can only defend, deflect, and rationalize. But the person who can say "I was wrong" and "I'll do better" becomes trustworthy—not because they never fail, but because they own their failures and learn from them.

Responsibility, in the end, is what makes you solid. It's what lets other people lean on you without fear that you'll collapse. It's what allows you to look at yourself in the mirror and respect what you see. It's what turns potential into purpose and intention into impact.

The culture may have turned away from responsibility, may have framed it as oppression or burden or outdated expectation. But the need for it hasn't changed. Every stable relationship depends on it. Every functional community requires it. Every meaningful life is built on it.

And it remains, as it always has been, freely available to anyone willing to claim it. Responsibility isn't something you're given. It's something you take. And the moment you take it—really take it, all the way down—you become someone worth knowing.

NINE

TRUTH

Truth is like the sun. You can shut it out for a time, but it ain't going away.
—Elvis Presley

Of all the words that have thinned in recent years, *truth* may be the most consequential. Not because it's used less—it's used constantly—but because it's been redefined in ways that gut its original meaning. We still hear the word everywhere: "Speak your truth." "Live your truth." "My truth is different from your truth." The word remains in circulation, but it no longer points to what it once pointed to.

Truth used to mean a solid connection to reality. A statement was true if it accurately described the way things actually are, regardless of whether anyone liked it, believed it, or found it convenient. Truth was objective—existing independent of human opinion, immune to manipulation, indifferent to our preferences. You couldn't make something true by believing it hard enough, and you couldn't make it false by refusing to acknowledge it. Truth simply was, and the task of honest people was to align their beliefs and their speech with it.

That understanding has fractured. Truth has been privatized, subjectivized, rendered into something closer to personal narrative than objective reality. "My truth" has become a common phrase, used to describe individual experience, personal perspective, or deeply felt conviction. And while experience and perspective matter—while subjective reality is real—the new usage has collapsed an essential distinction: the difference between *what I believe* and what is *true*.

This collapse didn't happen overnight. It accumulated through several shifts in how we think and talk about knowledge, identity, and authority.

The first shift was therapeutic. Psychology and counseling rightly recognized that people's subjective experiences matter, that feelings are real even when they're not rational, and that validating someone's interior world is part of helping them heal. "Your feelings are valid" became a therapeutic principle—and it's a good one, within its proper bounds. But the principle leaked out of clinical settings and into general discourse, where it morphed into "Your truth is valid." And once truth became a matter of validation rather than verification, objectivity started to erode.

The second shift was philosophical—a loss of confidence in the possibility of knowing objective truth at all – originating in universities and intellectual circles. Postmodern philosophy argued that all knowledge is shaped by perspective, power, and language, and that claims to objectivity are often masks for domination. There's something to this critique—people do use the language of objectivity to enforce their preferences, and marginalized perspectives have been excluded from what counts as "truth." But the critique was overcorrected. Instead of saying "we must be humble about our access to truth," many concluded "there is no truth, only perspectives." And once that conclusion took root, truth became a matter of whose perspective had more power.

The third shift was technological. Social media gave everyone a platform, which democratized speech in valuable ways but also created an environment where volume and virality often matter more than accuracy. A compelling personal story spreads faster than a careful argument. An emotionally charged claim gets more engagement than a nuanced correction. And in that environment, "my truth"—delivered with conviction and wrapped in personal experience—often outcompetes "the truth," which requires evidence, humility, and the willingness to be wrong.

The result is a culture where truth claims have become strangely toothless. People assert their truth, others assert theirs, and there's no shared framework for deciding between them. The assumption is that both can be true simultaneously, or that truth is simply a matter of perspective, or that insisting on objective truth is itself a kind of aggression—an attempt to impose your reality on someone else.

But reality doesn't negotiate.

In engineering, we have a saying: "Physics always wins." Or sometimes, "The laws of thermodynamics always win." It doesn't matter how elegant your design is, how much money you've spent, or how confident you are—if you've violated a physical law, the system will fail. Reality doesn't care about your intentions. It doesn't grade on a curve. The steam pressure is what it is. The load-bearing capacity is what it is. You can ignore it, but you can't change it.

Truth works the same way.

On January 28, 1986, the Space Shuttle Challenger broke apart 73 seconds after launch, killing all seven crew members. The cause was an O-ring seal that failed in cold temperatures. Engineers at Morton Thiokol had warned that launching in freezing conditions was dangerous—they had data showing the O-rings became brittle and lost elasticity below a certain temperature. But there was pressure to launch. The mission had already been delayed. There were political and public relations considerations. Managers and politicians wanted it to happen.

So they redefined the acceptable risk. They reinterpreted the data. They questioned the engineers' conclusions. They essentially treated the truth about O-ring performance as negotiable—as though reality would accommodate their deadline if they believed hard enough that it would.

Reality didn't accommodate. The O-ring failed exactly as the engineers predicted. Seven people died. The shuttle program was grounded for years. And no amount of post-accident rationalization could change what had happened.

This is what ignoring truth costs. Not hurt feelings. Not damaged relationships. Not even reputation. Sometimes it costs lives.

The same pattern repeats in smaller ways constantly. The business that ignores financial reality and insists everything is fine—until bankruptcy forces the truth into the open. The doctor who dismisses symptoms because they don't fit their diagnosis—until the patient's condition deteriorates past the point of treatment. The parent who refuses to acknowledge their child's addiction—until the overdose makes denial impossible. In every case, reality was there all along. It was waiting. And when truth finally forced its way back into view, the cost was higher than it would have been if anyone had acknowledged it earlier.

This is why truth cannot be personal or subjective when it comes to matters of fact. You can have your own feelings about the O-rings. You can have your own interpretation of what the failure means politically or culturally. But you can't have your own truth about whether they fail in cold temperatures. They either do or they don't. The temperature at launch was either within safe parameters or it wasn't. These aren't perspectives. They're facts. And facts don't care what you believe about them.

The engineering mindset understands this instinctively—because in engineering, you can't bluff reality. The bridge either holds or it collapses. The circuit either works or it doesn't. The calculation is either correct or the system fails and public safety is compromised. There's no negotiation, no appeal to sincerity, no points for creativity. There's only what is. And the engineer's job is to align their work with what is, not to reshape reality according to their preferences.

Human life requires the same rigor. Not because we're machines, but because we live in a world that operates according to principles we didn't create and can't revise. Truth isn't a constraint on human flourishing—it's the ground on which flourishing becomes possible.

Here's what the fragmentation of truth looks like in practice.

A person says, "I feel like you don't care about me." That's a statement about their subjective experience, and it's real—they genuinely feel that way. But whether you actually care is a separate question. You might care deeply but express it poorly. Their feeling is valid; their interpretation may not be accurate. Conflating the two—treating the feeling as equivalent to the fact—prevents clarity and makes resolution impossible.

Or consider classroom discussions where students are encouraged to "speak their truth" about historical events. A student says, "My truth is that Columbus was a hero." Another says, "My truth is that Columbus was a genocidal monster." Both are framed as equally valid perspectives. But historical truth isn't a matter of perspective—it's a matter of evidence. Columbus did specific things, documented in records, with measurable consequences. You can interpret those actions differently depending on your values, but the actions themselves are facts. Calling both interpretations "truths" obscures the difference between what happened and how we feel about it.

Or think about the common phrase "lived experience." It's used to elevate personal testimony over external evidence: "You can't argue with my lived experience." And in one sense, that's right—no one can tell you that you didn't experience what you experienced. But lived experience is interpretation, not raw data. Two people can experience the same event and interpret it completely differently. Their experiences are both real, but their interpretations aren't necessarily both true. Treating all lived experience as unassailable truth makes conversation impossible, because it eliminates the possibility of correction, nuance, or learning.

The fragmentation of truth creates several cascading problems.

First, it makes persuasion nearly impossible. If truth is subjective, then disagreement isn't about discovering what's real—it's about asserting competing perspectives. There's no reason to change your mind because your truth is as valid as anyone else's. Conversations stop being searches for understanding and become performances of identity. People don't argue to discover *truth*; they argue to defend *their truth*.

Second, it erodes trust. If everyone has their own truth, how do you know who to believe? When someone makes a factual claim, you have no way to evaluate it except by deciding whether you trust their perspective. And since perspectives are shaped by identity, ideology, and interest, trust collapses into tribalism. You believe people who share your identity and dismiss people who don't. Truth becomes a team sport. A wise English teacher used to explain judicious use of superlatives with the example, "If every baby is beautiful, no baby is beautiful." The same applies to truth. If every feeling or opinion is truth, then there is no truth.

Third, it disempowers the vulnerable. The powerful have always been able to assert their version of reality and make it stick. "Might makes right" is an old problem. But the solution isn't to say that everyone's truth is equally valid—it's to insist on objective truth and then hold the powerful accountable to it. When truth becomes subjective, the powerful benefit. They can dismiss inconvenient facts as "just your perspective" while asserting their own narrative as definitive. The weak, who depend on truth-telling to expose injustice, lose their most powerful weapon.

Fourth, it makes reality optional. If truth is whatever you believe, then belief becomes untethered from the world. People can assert things that are demonstrably false and defend them as "my truth." This isn't liberation—it's delusion. A society that can't agree on basic facts can't function. It can't solve problems, make decisions, or hold anyone accountable, because there's no shared reality to reference.

The collapse of shared truth is most visible—and most destructive—in relationships. Marriage, friendship, parenting, and work all depend on a shared understanding of reality. When that foundation cracks, the relationship can't hold.

Consider a marriage where both partners are operating from "their truth." The husband says, "My truth is that I'm a devoted father who provides for this family." The wife says, "My truth is that you're emotionally absent and prioritize work over us." If truth is subjective, both statements are valid. There's nothing to resolve—just two competing realities that coexist without touching.

But relationships can't function that way. Either the husband is present and engaged, or he's not. Either he prioritizes family, or he doesn't. His intentions matter—they're part of the story. But they're not the whole story. His actions are observable facts that exist independent of his self-perception. The time he spends at work is measurable. The conversations he has (or doesn't have) with his children are real events. These aren't perspectives. They're data points that can be examined, discussed, and evaluated.

When both partners retreat to "my truth," they've abandoned the shared project of understanding what's actually happening. They've chosen validation over clarity. And validation, while it feels better in the moment, doesn't solve anything.

The husband leaves the conversation still believing he's devoted. The wife leaves still feeling abandoned. Nothing changes because nothing was actually addressed.

The alternative is harder but productive: both partners must agree that there's a truth to be discovered, even if neither of them sees it perfectly. The husband must consider the possibility that his intentions don't match his impact. The wife must consider the possibility that her interpretation doesn't account for constraints she's not seeing. Both are required to bring evidence—specific instances, patterns over time, measurable facts—and both, then, must be willing to revise their understanding when the evidence contradicts their assumptions.

This doesn't mean feelings don't matter. The wife's feeling of abandonment is real and deserves attention. But "I feel abandoned" is different from "You are abandoning us." The first is subjective experience that needs to be heard. The second is a factual claim that needs to be examined. Good relationships hold both: they honor subjective experience while insisting on objective accuracy.

The same dynamic appears in every relationship. The parent who insists "My truth is that I'm supportive" while their child experiences constant criticism. The employee who claims "My truth is that I work hard" while their output consistently misses deadlines. The friend who says "My truth is that I'm always there for you" while repeatedly canceling plans. In each case, the person has mistaken their self-image for reality.

This isn't about who's right. It's about whether there's even a shared standard for determining what's right. And without that standard, relationships become echo chambers where everyone just reinforces their own narrative. You can't repair what you won't acknowledge. You can't improve what you won't measure. You can't love someone well if you refuse to see them accurately.

The language of "my truth" sounds compassionate—it seems to honor everyone's experience equally. But it's actually a form of relational abandonment. It says: "Your reality and mine don't have to connect. We can both be right even when we contradict each other. There's no shared world we're both trying to understand—just separate experiences we're each entitled to."

That might work for acquaintances or strangers whose lives don't intersect much. It's catastrophic for anyone who actually depends on others. Parents and children inhabit the same reality—the child's development, the family's resources, the consequences of decisions are all objective facts that both parties need to see clearly. Spouses inhabit the same reality—the state of the marriage, the distribution of labor, the health of the relationship are all things that exist independent of either person's feelings about them.

Truth in relationships isn't a weapon. It's a gift. It's what allows two people to stop talking past each other and start talking to each other. It's what makes repair possible because you can't fix what you won't name. And it's what makes growth possible because you can't change what you won't acknowledge.

When couples come back from the edge of divorce, it's almost always because they stopped defending their competing truths and started investigating the actual truth. When friendships recover from betrayal, it's because someone told the truth about what happened instead of spinning a more comfortable narrative. When parents and children reconcile after years of distance, it's because someone finally said what was real instead of what was safe.

Shared truth is the price of admission for any relationship that matters. And once you've paid that price, you discover it wasn't a cost—it was an investment. Because the ground you're standing on is solid now. And solid ground is the only place you can build anything that lasts.

Elvis Presley's line, unlikely as it sounds for someone whose art was about feeling rather than philosophy, captures the essential point: *truth doesn't care whether you acknowledge it.* You can shut it out, ignore it, redefine it, or call it your enemy. But it remains. And eventually, it reasserts itself—often at great cost to the people who spent too long pretending it didn't exist.

So how do we recover truth?

First, we restore the distinction between subjective experience and objective reality. Your feelings are real. Your perspective matters. Your experience deserves respect. But none of that makes your interpretation automatically true. Truth is what corresponds to reality, and reality exists whether you perceive it or not.

This doesn't mean dismissing people's experiences. It means helping people distinguish between "I felt hurt" (subjective, real, valid) and "You intended to hurt me" (an interpretation that may or may not be true). It means recognizing that two people can have different experiences of the same event, but that doesn't mean there are two different truths about what happened—it means we need to investigate further.

Second, we recover humility about our access to truth. None of us sees reality perfectly. We all have blind spots, biases, and limitations. This is why truth-seeking is a communal activity—we need other perspectives to correct our errors. But humility about our access to truth is not the same as denying truth's existence. Saying "I might be wrong" is different from saying "there's no right answer." The first is wisdom. The second is surrender.

Third, we must insist that evidence matters. Not all claims are equally valid. Some correspond to reality; others don't. And we have ways—imperfect but real—of distinguishing between them. We can look at data. We can test predictions. We can examine consistency. We can ask whether a claim fits with what else we know. This doesn't give us certainty, but it gives us direction. And it prevents truth from collapsing entirely into power.

Fourth, we have to recover the courage to say "That's not true." Not "I disagree with you" or "That's not my experience," but "That's objectively false." This has become hard because it sounds arrogant or dismissive. But sometimes disagreement isn't about perspective—it's about one person being wrong. And if we can't name falsehood when we encounter it, we've lost the ability to defend truth.

Fifth, we stop treating "your truth" as a synonym for "truth". The phrase sounds generous, but it's actually condescending. It implies that your version of reality doesn't need to correspond to anyone else's, that accuracy doesn't matter, that you're entitled to your own facts. Real respect means taking people seriously enough to tell them when they're wrong—not because you're superior, but because truth matters and you believe they're capable of recognizing it.

Finally, we strive to remember why truth matters. It's not an abstract philosophical principle. It's the foundation of every relationship, every institution, every shared endeavor. Without truth, trust is impossible. Without truth, justice is impossible. Without truth, progress is impossible. A lie might be comforting in the moment, but it always exacts a cost—and that cost is paid in confusion, conflict, and the slow erosion of everything we depend on to live together.

Truth doesn't guarantee happiness. It often brings discomfort. It can shatter illusions we'd prefer to keep. It demands that we change our minds when the evidence shifts. It humbles us by showing how often we're wrong. But it's also the only solid ground we have. Everything else—ideology, emotion, preference, identity—shifts with circumstance. Truth remains.

This doesn't mean we'll ever grasp truth perfectly. We won't. Human knowledge is always incomplete, always provisional, always open to revision. But the fact that we see imperfectly doesn't mean there's nothing to see. The fact that we understand partially doesn't mean there's nothing to understand. The goal isn't omniscience—it's honesty. The commitment to describe reality as accurately as we can, to correct our errors when they're revealed, and to resist the temptation to reshape the world according to our wishes.

In the end, truth isn't something we create. It's something we discover—slowly, imperfectly, but really. And the more we align ourselves with it, the more solid our lives become. Not because truth makes everything easy, but because truth is the only foundation that doesn't crumble under pressure.

We can call it "my truth" if we want. We can soften it, personalize it, make it feel less demanding. But the world will keep being what it is. And sooner or later, we are forced to decide whether we want to live in that world or keep pretending we can invent our own.

Ten

HUMILITY

Humility is not thinking less of yourself; it's thinking of yourself less.
—C.S. Lewis

Humility has become the virtue no one wants. In a culture that celebrates self-confidence, self-promotion, and self-assertion, humility sounds like weakness. It sounds like letting yourself be walked on, like settling for less than you deserve, like a failure to advocate for yourself in a world that rewards loudness.

But that understanding of humility is wrong. It confuses humility with timidity, with self-deprecation, with the kind of false modesty that's really just fishing for compliments. Real humility isn't about thinking you're worthless. It's about having an accurate sense of both your strengths and your limitations. It's about recognizing that you're not the center of the universe, that other people's perspectives have value, and that you don't know everything—even about things you know a lot about.

Humility used to mean accurate self-assessment. It was the virtue that kept you honest about yourself—neither inflating your importance nor denying your genuine strengths. A humble person could acknowledge what they were good at without arrogance and admit what they didn't know without shame. Humility was what prevented competence from becoming arrogance and confidence from becoming delusion.

That understanding has been lost. Humility now gets confused with a cluster of things it was never meant to be: low self-esteem, excessive self-criticism, the inability to stand up for yourself, or the habit of minimizing your achievements to avoid seeming proud. These aren't humility—they're dysfunctions that sometimes wear humility's name.

The confusion comes partly from how humility has been weaponized. "Be humble" often means "don't challenge me" or "accept your place" or "stop advocating for yourself." This is especially true in hierarchical systems where those in power benefit from others staying quiet. When humility becomes a tool for keeping people in their place, no wonder people reject it.

But rejecting false humility doesn't mean rejecting the real thing. Because real humility is essential—not just for moral character, but for basic functioning in a complex world. Without humility, you can't learn. You can't admit mistakes. You can't receive criticism. You can't recognize when you're wrong. You become unteachable, unbearable, and eventually, incompetent.

Here's what humility actually is: it's the recognition that your perspective is limited, that your knowledge is incomplete, and that you might be wrong about things you're confident about. This doesn't mean you can't hold strong convictions. It means you hold them with the awareness that you're a fallible human being whose understanding is shaped by limited experience and imperfect reasoning.

Humility is what allows you to say "I don't know" without feeling like you've failed. It's what allows you to say "I was wrong" without feeling like you've lost status. It's what allows you to listen to criticism without immediately getting defensive. It's what allows you to learn from people who know less than you about most things but know more than you about this particular thing.

In engineering and in the military, humility isn't optional—it's survival. The engineer who's too proud to double-check their calculations will eventually design something that fails. The officer who's too arrogant to listen to the sergeant with field experience will get people killed. In environments where reality has consequences, humility isn't a nice-to-have virtue. It's a requirement.

But outside those environments—in places where consequences arrive slowly or are easily blamed on others—humility has become rare. Corporate executives who refuse to admit mistakes, politicians who never acknowledge error, public intellectuals who treat every criticism as persecution, social media users who proclaim opinions with absolute certainty on topics they learned about ten minutes ago. The pattern is everywhere: certainty without expertise, confidence without competence, assertions without evidence.

The opposite of humility isn't confidence—it's arrogance. And arrogance is just certainty that outpaces knowledge. The arrogant person doesn't know more than the humble person. They're just more certain about what they think they know. And that certainty makes them dangerous, because it prevents them from recognizing their errors until the damage is done.

Consider how this plays out in practice.

A manager receives feedback that their communication style is creating problems for the team. The humble manager listens, asks clarifying questions, and considers whether the feedback might be accurate. They might not agree with all of it, but they take it seriously. The arrogant manager dismisses it immediately—the team is too sensitive, they don't understand the pressure the manager is under, they need to toughen up. The arrogant manager learns nothing, the problems persist, and eventually good people leave.

Or consider two experts in the same field. One has genuine humility—they know their area of expertise deeply, but they also know how much they don't know, how much their conclusions depend on assumptions that might be wrong, how much their field still doesn't understand. The other expert has arrogance disguised as expertise—they speak with complete certainty, dismiss contrary evidence, and treat questions as attacks. The first expert is more trustworthy precisely because they're more honest about the limits of their knowledge.

Or think about how people engage with political and moral questions. The humble person recognizes that complex issues rarely have simple answers, that people who disagree might have reasons worth considering, that their own understanding is shaped by their particular experiences and might be missing important perspectives. The arrogant person has it all figured out—anyone who disagrees is either stupid or evil, complexity is just an excuse for avoiding clear moral positions, and their own political tribe has a monopoly on truth.

The first person can learn, can change their mind, can engage productively with people who see things differently. The second person can't. They're locked into their current understanding, unable to grow because they can't admit they might need to.

Humility also has a social dimension that's been lost. In a healthy community, people practice mutual humility—recognizing that everyone has something to contribute, that wisdom isn't the exclusive property of the educated or the powerful, that sometimes the person who knows least about most things knows most about this particular thing.

But contemporary culture sorts people into categories—expert and ignorant, educated and uneducated, enlightened and backwards—and assumes that wisdom flows in only one direction. The expert has nothing to learn from the layperson. The educated have nothing to learn from the uneducated. The progressive has nothing to learn from the traditional. This isn't humility—it's credentialism masquerading as expertise.

Real humility recognizes that knowledge is distributed. The person with a doctorate degree in public policy might understand theory but not how policies actually affect people on the ground. The person who's lived in a community for decades might not know the academic literature but knows what's worked and what hasn't in practice. Both kinds of knowledge matter. And the humble person—whether they're the expert or the resident—recognizes this.

The recovery of humility requires several things.

First, let's agree to separate humility from weakness. Humility isn't the inability to stand up for yourself. It's the ability to assess yourself accurately. A humble person can be confident when they're on solid ground and uncertain when they're not. They can assert their competence in areas where they're actually competent and defer to others in areas where they're not. This isn't weakness—it's honesty.

Second, we must recover the habit of saying "I don't know." This is harder than it sounds. In a culture that rewards certainty and punishes uncertainty, admitting ignorance feels like losing status. But "I don't know" is often the most honest answer available. And it's the beginning of learning. The person who can't say

"I don't know" can't learn, because learning requires admitting there's something you don't know yet.

Third, we need to practice intellectual humility—the recognition that our understanding is always incomplete and might be wrong. This doesn't mean abandoning all convictions or pretending that truth is relative. It means holding convictions with the awareness that you're a fallible person, that smarter people than you have been wrong about things they were certain about, and that confidence isn't the same as correctness.

Fourth, stop treating disagreement as evidence of stupidity or malice. When someone disagrees with you, the humble response is to ask why—to try to understand their reasoning, to see if they know something you don't, to consider whether your position might have weaknesses you haven't noticed. The arrogant response is to dismiss them without engaging with their actual arguments. The first response sometimes leads to learning. The second never does.

Fifth, we need to recover the practice of apologizing—actually apologizing, not the non-apology of "I'm sorry you feel that way." An apology requires humility because it requires admitting you were wrong, that you caused harm, and that you need to do better. People who can't apologize aren't strong—they're fragile. They're so insecure that they can't admit error without feeling like they've lost status. But actually, the opposite is true: the person who can admit fault and genuinely apologize earns respect, because everyone knows how hard it is to do that.

Finally, it is imperative that we recognize that humility doesn't mean treating all opinions as equally valid. Humility isn't relativism. It's possible to be both humble and certain—certain about some things while remaining open to correction about others, confident in your knowledge while recognizing its limits. The humble expert knows what they know and knows what they don't know. The arrogant expert doesn't make that distinction.

Humility is also what makes other virtues sustainable. Courage without humility becomes recklessness. Justice without humility becomes self-righteousness.

Truth-seeking without humility becomes dogmatism. Every virtue, pressed too far without the moderating influence of humility, becomes a vice.

This is why Lewis's definition is so precise: *"Humility is not thinking less of yourself; it's thinking of yourself less."* The humble person isn't constantly performing self-deprecation or dwelling on their flaws. They're just not preoccupied with themselves. They can think about other people, other perspectives, other possibilities, because their attention isn't consumed by defending or promoting their own ego.

The person without humility spends enormous energy managing their image, defending their reputation, and nursing their sense of grievance when they don't get sufficient recognition. The humble person is freed from all that. They can focus on the work, on other people, on what actually needs doing, because they're not constantly monitoring how they're being perceived.

This freedom is one of humility's great gifts. The arrogant person is a slave to their ego—always needing validation, always sensitive to slights, always performing competence even when they're uncertain. The humble person is free from all that. They can admit what they don't know. They can ask for help. They can learn from anyone. They can change their minds without feeling like they've lost something.

There's also a kind of humility that comes from suffering—not the kind that breaks you, but the kind that teaches you that you're not in control, that you need other people, that you're more fragile than you thought. People who've been broken and rebuilt often carry a different kind of humility—not because they think less of themselves, but because they've learned how much they depend on things beyond themselves.

This isn't the humility of low self-esteem. It's the humility of reality. You can't control as much as you thought. You can't earn your way out of every problem. You can't maintain your life through willpower alone. You need help, you need grace, you need other people. And recognizing that doesn't diminish you—it situates you accurately in a world that's larger and more complex than any individual can master.

The contemporary resistance to humility comes partly from confusing it with *humiliation*. But these are opposites. Humiliation is what someone else does to you—an assault on your dignity. Humility is what you practice yourself—an honest assessment of your limits. Humiliation diminishes you. Humility actually protects your dignity, because it prevents you from overreaching in ways that will eventually expose you.

The person who pretends to know more than they do will eventually be found out. The person who refuses to admit mistakes will eventually be caught in a mistake they can't deny. The person who won't accept feedback will eventually alienate everyone around them. Arrogance produces these outcomes. Humility prevents them.

So the question isn't whether you'll be humbled—it's whether you'll practice humility before life forces it on you. Because reality has a way of teaching humility to people who won't learn it voluntarily. The engineer who won't double-check will eventually see their design fail. The manager who won't listen will eventually lose their best people. The person who won't admit error will eventually make an error too big to ignore.

You can learn humility the easy way—by practicing it, by admitting what you don't know, by listening to people who know things you don't—or you can learn it the hard way, when reality forces you to confront how much you got wrong. But one way or another, you'll learn it. Because reality doesn't care about your ego.

The recovery of humility, then, is also the recovery of *honesty*—not just honesty about the world, but honesty about yourself. Who you actually are, not who you wish you were. What you actually know, not what you wish you knew. Where you actually stand, not where you wish you stood.

This honesty is painful at first. It requires admitting things you'd rather not admit—that you were wrong, that you need help, that you're not as competent as you thought. But on the other side of that pain is freedom. The freedom to learn. The freedom to grow. The freedom to be honestly yourself instead of defending an inflated version of yourself.

Humility doesn't make you smaller. It makes you real. And in a world full of performance, pretense, and inflated self-regard, being real is both rare and necessary.

Because the alternative—a culture where no one can admit error, where everyone performs certainty they don't feel, where disagreement is treated as personal attack—is unbearable. And we're already living in it.

The recovery starts with the willingness to say three words that have become almost impossible: "I was wrong." Not "mistakes were made." Not "I'm sorry you feel that way." Not "I'm sorry if anyone was offended." Just: "I was wrong." And then: "I'll do better."

That's humility. That's what it sounds like. That's what makes learning possible, what makes relationships repairable, what makes wisdom attainable. It's not weakness. It's not self-deprecation. It's not letting yourself be walked on. It's just honesty about who you are and what you know. And it's the beginning of becoming who you could be.

ELEVEN

REVERENCE

The world is charged with the grandeur of God.
—Gerard Manley Hopkins

Reverence is one of those words that sounds archaic the moment you say it. It belongs to another era—Victorian parlors, stone cathedrals, formal ceremonies attended by people in uncomfortable clothing. It feels stiff, pious, distant from ordinary life. Most people today wouldn't describe themselves as reverent, and if pressed, they might not even be sure what the word means anymore.

The degradation of reverence is most visible in two words that used to carry real weight: *awesome* and *amazing*.

Awesome once meant exactly what it sounds like—inspiring awe. It described realities so vast or powerful that they produced a kind of reverent terror: God, the ocean in a storm, the night sky, the moment of birth or death. Awesome was rare because genuinely awe-inspiring experiences are rare. You didn't encounter the awesome casually. You encountered it at the edges of human experience, in moments when you were reminded of your smallness and the world's magnitude.

Now awesome means "pretty good." Your lunch was awesome. The parking spot you found was awesome. The new season of a TV show is awesome. We've taken a word that used to describe encountering the transcendent and made it a synonym for "nice." And in doing so, we've lost the language for the experiences the word was meant to name.

Amazing has suffered the same fate. To be amazed meant to be struck with wonder, stopped in your tracks by something so unexpected or magnificent that your normal categories of understanding couldn't contain it. The Grand Canyon is amazing. A total solar eclipse is amazing. Watching your child take their first steps is amazing. These are experiences that genuinely astonish—that rupture the ordinary and leave you changed.

But now everything is amazing. The coffee is amazing. The hotel room is amazing. Someone's haircut is amazing. We've inflated the word to the point where it no longer means anything more than "I approve" or "this met my expectations." And when everything is amazing, nothing is. We've spent the currency of wonder on trivialities.

This isn't just linguistic pedantry. When you lose the words for awe and amazement, you lose the capacity to experience them fully. Language doesn't just describe reality—it shapes what you're able to perceive. If "awesome" and "amazing" are always available for ordinary experiences, you have no words left when you encounter something genuinely transcendent. You're left saying "that was really, really awesome" or "truly amazing," trying desperately to elevate language that's already been flattened.

The result is that younger generations no longer have vocabulary for reverence. They've inherited a language where the words that used to mark significance have been reduced to intensifiers for mild approval. When they stand at the edge of the Grand Canyon or hold a newborn or witness something that should produce awe, they reach for words that have already been exhausted. "That's so awesome," they say—using the same words they used for a burrito an hour earlier. The experience deserves more, but the language isn't there anymore.

That's the loss this chapter is about. Not the word—the thing the word was built to carry.

But reverence isn't about formality or religious ritual, not God or gods. At its core, reverence is the recognition that something exists beyond yourself—something larger, deeper, higher—that deserves a particular kind of attention. It's the instinct to lower your voice in the presence of mystery. It's the sense that some moments, some places, some realities should not be treated casually. Reverence is what you feel when you encounter something so significant that flippancy would be a betrayal.

We still experience this, even if we've lost the vocabulary for it. Continue with the examples I introduced above. Standing at the rim of the Grand Canyon. Holding a newborn child. Watching the sun rise after a long, dark night. Sitting in silence after someone speaks a truth that cuts through all the noise. These moments have weight. They ask something of us—not compliance, not worship, but a kind of attentiveness that acknowledges we're in the presence of something that exceeds our ability to fully grasp it.

That attentiveness is reverence. And it's nearly extinct. Barfield would say the word has thinned because the experience it names has thinned—that we've lost the word because we've lost the thing, and we've lost the thing because we've lost the word.

The modern world, especially in Western cultures, is suspicious of reverence. Suspicious of anything that suggests hierarchy—not of people over people, but of some realities over others. We've been trained to see everything as equal, to resist the idea that some experiences or truths might be more significant than others. Irony has become our default register, a protective distance we maintain so we're never caught taking anything too seriously. If you speak reverently about something, you risk sounding naive, unsophisticated, or worst of all, sincere.

But a life without reverence is a flat life. When nothing is sacred, everything becomes trivial. When no moment demands your full attention, no moment receives it. When you can't distinguish between what matters and what doesn't, you lose the ability to respond appropriately to anything. Reverence creates altitude. It establishes heights. It reminds us that the world isn't all one level, that some things—truth, beauty, love, sacrifice—stand above the ordinary and deserve to be approached differently.

The loss of reverence didn't happen through a single decision. It accumulated through a series of cultural shifts, each reasonable on its own but collectively corrosive.

One shift was the democratization of access. Technology made everything available, instantly, at no cost. You can listen to a symphony while scrolling your phone. You can see the Sistine Chapel on a screen while eating lunch. You can read Shakespeare on a website cluttered with ads. Accessibility is good—art and beauty and knowledge should be available to everyone. But when everything is available all the time, nothing feels special. The effort required to encounter something used to be part of what made it significant. Now that effort is gone, and with it, some of the reverence.

Another shift was the collapse of shared moral frameworks. Reverence depends on agreement about what's worth revering. When communities shared beliefs—about God or a higher power, about nature, about human dignity—they naturally developed practices of reverence around those beliefs. But we no longer share much. Pluralism is valuable, but it's also destabilizing. When every perspective is considered equally valid, it becomes hard to say that anything in particular deserves reverence. We're left with a kind of moral relativism where the only thing we all agree on is that no one should tell anyone else what to revere.

A third shift was the rise of entertainment as the dominant mode of engagement. Entertainment is designed to be consumable, disposable, always moving. It keeps you stimulated but never asks you to stop and dwell. Reverence, by contrast, requires stillness. It requires you to be present long enough for awe to develop. But we've trained ourselves to scroll, swipe, skip—to treat every experience as content to be consumed and discarded. In that environment, reverence becomes impossible. You can't revere what you're already moving past.

And perhaps most significantly, irony became the tone of cultural sophistication. To be smart, you had to be detached. To be cool, you had to be unimpressed. Earnestness became cringe. Sincerity became suspect. If you expressed wonder or awe without undercutting it with a joke, you risked looking foolish. So people learned to protect themselves by mocking before they could be mocked. The cost of that protection is enormous: you can't revere what you're busy making fun of.

Winston Churchill understood this. When Churchill—himself a "great man"—wrote about great men and the great events they influenced in *Great Con-*

temporaries—Roosevelt, T.E. Lawrence, Clemenceau, Balfour—he wrote with respect proportionate to their stature. He didn't need to diminish them to seem sophisticated. He didn't undercut praise with irony to protect himself from seeming naive. He could write sentences like "Here was a man worthy of honor" without flinching, without apologizing, without softening it with a joke. That wasn't servility or hero worship. That was the recognition that some people and some events merit serious treatment, and that giving them that treatment doesn't make you unsophisticated—it makes you capable of recognizing greatness when you encounter it.

Modern writers can't do this anymore. We've trained ourselves to deflate everything—especially anything that might be called great. If you write seriously about someone's courage or sacrifice or achievement, you sound earnest in the worst sense. Reviewers will call you "hagiographic" or "uncritical." The acceptable move is to acknowledge greatness while simultaneously noting flaws, contradictions, and failures—as though serious treatment requires equal-time criticism to prove you're not a sucker. But Churchill knew something we've forgotten: you can see a person's flaws and still write about their greatness with reverence. The two don't cancel each other out. Greatness is real. And it deserves language adequate to it.

Or think about how we engage with beauty. A great piece of music used to stop people in their tracks. Now it's background noise while we work or exercise. A stunning landscape used to inspire pilgrimage. Now it's a photo opportunity—something to capture and post rather than something to dwell in. Beauty hasn't disappeared, but our capacity to revere it has diminished. We see it, we acknowledge it, we move on. We rarely let it change us.

This is what happens when a culture loses reverence: it loses the ability to distinguish between the significant and the trivial, between what deserves careful attention and what can be casually consumed. Everything flattens to the same level. And at that level, nothing can be genuinely awesome because awesome has been democratized into meaninglessness.

The same is true of truth, of courage, of sacrifice, of any reality that once carried moral or spiritual weight. We've flattened them all. We've made them accessible, consumable, optional. And in doing so, we've lost the sense that some things should be approached with awe rather than casual interest.

But reverence isn't nostalgia. It's not about returning to old rituals or pretending that traditional forms of piety are the only valid expressions of it. Reverence is a human instinct, available to anyone regardless of belief system. You don't have to be religious to revere something. You just have to recognize that some experiences, some truths, some moments transcend your ability to control or fully comprehend them—and that the appropriate response is humility, attention, and a kind of wonder.

So how do we recover reverence in a culture that's forgotten how?

We start by practicing stillness. Reverence can't develop in constant motion. It requires you to stop long enough for something to register as significant. This doesn't mean adopting a monastic lifestyle. It means creating small pockets of quiet—moments where you're not consuming, producing, or performing, but simply present.

Second, resist the reflex to ironize everything. Irony is useful—it protects against fanaticism, exposes hypocrisy, and keeps earnestness from becoming oppressive. But when irony becomes your only mode, you lose access to the experiences that make life meaningful. Sometimes the appropriate response to something beautiful or true or good is simply to acknowledge it, without the protective distance of a joke.

Third, teach it. Children won't develop reverence by accident. They'll learn it by watching adults treat certain things with care, by being brought into moments that matter and taught how to inhabit them. This means not rushing through ceremonies, not treating every occasion as casual, not allowing every environment to be loud and chaotic. It means occasionally saying, "This is important. Pay attention."

Fourth, allow for the sacred again. Not necessarily in religious terms—though for many people, religion is where reverence is most naturally cultivated—but in the recognition that some things are set apart. A moment of silence. A vow spoken publicly. A truth spoken in the presence of grief. These aren't just nice gestures—they're acts of reverence that remind us we're part of something larger than ourselves.

Recovering reverence also means recovering the distinction between the sacred and the profane. Not in a moralistic sense—this is holy, that is sinful—but in the recognition that not everything deserves the same treatment. A joke at a funeral isn't funny; it's a violation of tone. Casual chatter during a solemn moment isn't friendly; it's disrespectful. These aren't arbitrary rules—they're recognition that some contexts demand a different register of speech and behavior.

Children understand this instinctively. They sense when a moment is serious even if they can't articulate why. They lower their voices. They pay attention. They respond to weight. But they lose that instinct if adults don't model it, if every moment is treated with the same casual cheerfulness, if nothing is ever held as too important to joke about.

Reverence is also what protects things from being cheapened. When you revere something, you handle it carefully. You don't use it carelessly. You don't mock it or reduce it. This applies to ideas, to relationships, to traditions. A person who reveres marriage treats it differently than someone who sees it as a contract that can be dissolved when it stops being convenient. A person who reveres truth treats it differently than someone who treats it as a tool for winning arguments. Reverence creates boundaries that protect what's valuable from degradation.

And reverence has a political dimension, though not in the partisan sense. A society that can't revere anything becomes ungovernable, because reverence is what makes people willing to sacrifice for something larger than themselves. Reverence for justice makes people pursue it even when it's costly. Reverence for freedom makes people defend it even when it's inconvenient. Reverence for human dignity makes people protect it even when they disagree with the person in question. Without reverence, politics becomes pure self-interest—everyone grabbing what they can, no one willing to subordinate their desires to the common good.

Finally, stop treating reverence as weakness. The person who can't revere anything isn't sophisticated—they're impoverished. They're missing the capacity to respond fully to the world. Reverence doesn't make you gullible or naive. It makes you capable of depth. It makes you able to encounter greatness without needing to diminish it.

Recovering reverence means recovering the ability to stop. To be still. To let something matter without needing to process it, critique it, or turn it into content. It means allowing certain moments to be heavy, certain truths to be awesome in the old sense—full of awe, not just impressive.

Gerard Manley Hopkins wrote that the world is "charged with the grandeur of God." You don't have to share his theology to sense the truth he's pointing toward: the world contains more significance than we can exhaust, more beauty than we can comprehend, more mystery than we can solve. That recognition—that we're surrounded by realities that exceed us—is what reverence is.

And when we lose it, we don't become more free or more enlightened. We just become smaller.

A life without reverence is a life lived entirely on the surface, where nothing penetrates, nothing transforms, nothing demands more than passing attention. It's a life that skims but never dives. A life that sees but never marvels. A life that knows but never wonders.

That's not sophistication. That's not maturity. That's not progress. It's just loss. And what's lost is the ability to live fully in a world that's far larger, stranger, and more astonishing than any of us will ever completely understand.

Tolkien had a word for what reverence does when it works—not the loss of it, but the recovery. In his essay *On Fairy-Stories*, he called it *recovery*—the restoration of clear sight after familiarity has dulled our perception. We stop seeing things as they actually are because we've grown too accustomed to them. The tree we pass every morning becomes invisible. The person we love most becomes predictable. The sky we live under becomes ceiling rather than canopy. Recovery, Tolkien argued, is what happens when something—a story, a piece of music, a moment of genuine beauty—strips away that familiarity and returns us to first sight. We see the tree again. We see the person again. We see the sky for what it actually is: a fact so astonishing that no one who truly looked at it could remain unmoved.

That is what reverence does. It recovers the world. It restores the appropriate weight to things that have been handled so casually they've become invisible. It doesn't ask you to pretend you're encountering something for the first time—it asks you to see it as if you were, which is harder and more valuable. The person who can still be stopped by the Grand Canyon after the tenth visit has something the person stopped only on the first visit never developed: the practiced discipline of seeing what's actually there.

Reverence opens the door to that world. And the person who can still walk through it—who can still be stopped in their tracks by something so significant that words fail—is the one still capable of living at the heights.

Twelve

ATTENTION

We become what we pay attention to.
—William James

Attention used to be something you gave. It was active, deliberate, costly. "Pay attention" wasn't just an instruction—it was a recognition that attention is valuable, that it can be spent or saved, that directing it toward something requires effort and choice. The metaphor of payment was precise: attention was currency, and you decided where to invest it.

Now attention is something that gets taken. Captured. Harvested. Algorithms compete for it. Devices demand it. The entire digital economy is built on extracting your attention and selling it to advertisers. We still use the word constantly—attention span, attention deficit, pay attention—but we've stopped understanding what it actually means. Attention isn't just noticing something. It's the sustained capacity to dwell with something long enough for it to become meaningful. And that capacity is vanishing.

The result isn't just distraction. It's the thinning of interior life itself. There's a kind of silence that's become rare—not the absence of noise, but the presence of inwardness. The quiet that allows a person to hear their own thoughts without distraction, to dwell quietly with an idea long enough for it to develop, to sit with a feeling until it reveals what it means. That silence used to be ordinary. Now it's almost impossible to find.

Most people today live in a state of constant interruption. Devices ping. Notifications arrive. Screens glow. The mind never settles. Even in moments that should be quiet—waiting in line, sitting alone, lying in bed before sleep—people reach for their phones, filling the gap with content, with noise, with anything that prevents them from being alone with themselves.

This matters more than it seems. The interior life is where meaning is made. It's where experience gets interpreted, where values are clarified, where identity takes shape. Without it, people begin to feel hollow—not because they lack experiences, but because they lack the capacity to absorb them. Life happens to them rather than in them. They react but don't reflect. They feel but don't understand. They move through days that blur into one another, vaguely aware that something is missing but unable to name what it is.

What's missing is depth. And depth requires attention.

William James understood this more than a century ago: "*We become what we pay attention to.*" Not what we intend to become, not what we wish we were, but what actually occupies our minds over time. Attention shapes perception, and perception shapes reality—at least the version of reality we inhabit. If your attention is constantly fragmented, pulled in a dozen directions at once, your inner world will be fragmented too. If your attention is shallow, skimming surfaces without ever going deep, your thoughts will be shallow. If your attention is always elsewhere, never fully present, you'll become a stranger to your own life.

The collapse of attention didn't happen through a single event. It accumulated through a series of shifts, each individually manageable but collectively devastating.

The first shift was technological. Devices were designed to capture attention and hold it. Algorithms learned what keeps people scrolling, clicking, watching. The goal wasn't to enhance life but to *maximize engagement*, which is a polite way of saying *addiction*. And it worked. The average person now checks their phone dozens of times a day, often without conscious intent.

I carry two mobile phones. One is for family—adult children scattered across three states, my wife's children in two others, and—don't forget—grandchildren and aging parents. The other is for work, where I'm subject to being called at any time. I've set personal boundaries about where I will and won't carry that second phone, but the first one is always with me. It has to be. This isn't addiction or weakness—it's the reality of modern family life spread across geography. But the cost is real. Even with the best intentions, even with legitimate reasons, constant accessibility means constant low-level vigilance. Part of my attention is always reserved for the possibility of interruption. The interior quiet that used to be ordinary is now something I have to fight for.

The mind has been trained to seek stimulation constantly, to feel restless without it, to interpret boredom as a problem that requires immediate solution.

The second shift was cultural. Busy-ness became a status symbol. Being constantly occupied, constantly connected, constantly productive became a sign of importance. People began to wear exhaustion and constant connectivity as a badge of honor, as though rest were weakness and stillness were laziness. The idea that a person might need unstructured time to think, to process, to simply be—that began to sound self-indulgent or impractical.

The third shift was educational. Schools increasingly structured every minute of a child's day, eliminating unstructured time, recess, free play—the spaces where imagination and relationship used to develop. How many of us declared our love to someone for the first time on the playground in elementary school? Children have now learned to expect constant direction, constant stimulation, constant supervision. They never developed the capacity to be alone with their thoughts because they were never given the chance.

And the fourth shift was social. Silence became uncomfortable. When conversation lagged, people filled it with their phones. When alone, people filled the silence with podcasts, music, videos—anything to avoid the discomfort of their own company. The interior life requires solitude, but solitude has become something people actively avoid.

The cost of these shifts is hard to measure because it's mostly invisible. People don't walk around naming what's been lost. They just feel vaguely anxious, vaguely restless, vaguely disconnected from themselves. They scroll when they're bored. They binge when they're sad. They keep moving because stopping feels dangerous. They mistake motion for purpose and stimulation for meaning.

But depth doesn't come from motion. It comes from stillness. It comes from the willingness to be present with yourself long enough for the noise to settle and the signal to emerge.

Here's what the loss of interior life looks like in practice.

A person experiences something difficult—a conflict with a friend, a disappointment at work, a moment of grief. In an earlier era, they might have walked, sat quietly, written in a journal (or tried writing a book), or simply stared out the window while their mind worked through it. The processing happened slowly, organically, with time for nuance and complexity. Now, the same person immediately reaches for distraction. They scroll social media, watch videos, text someone, listen to a podcast. The difficult feeling is avoided rather than processed. And because it's avoided, it never resolves. It just accumulates, along with all the other unprocessed emotions, creating a kind of emotional static that makes everything feel harder than it should.

Or consider a person trying to form an opinion about something complicated. In a world with interior life, they'd read, think, reconsider, read more, sit with the tension of not knowing, and eventually arrive at a position they'd tested against their own values and experience. Now, they read a headline, see what others are saying, align themselves with the tribe that feels most familiar, and adopt that position without ever subjecting it to real scrutiny. The opinion isn't theirs—it's borrowed. But because they've never developed the habit of deep thinking, they don't notice the difference.

Or think about someone who feels they've lost a sense of who they are. They can't name their values, don't know what they truly want, feel like they're just going through motions. That loss of self isn't mysterious—it's the result of never spending time alone with themselves. Identity isn't something you're born with fully formed. It's something you discover through reflection, through asking hard questions, through sitting with confusion until clarity emerges. But if you're never alone, never quiet, never still, that work doesn't happen. You remain a stranger to yourself.

The fragmentation of attention also damages language. Words depend on the ability to hold a thought long enough to find the right one. Writing depends on the ability to sustain focus through complexity. Conversation depends on the ability to listen without planning your next sentence. All of these require attention—sustained, disciplined, uninterrupted attention. And that's exactly what's vanished.

Consider what happens when you read a book like you're doing now—an actual book, not an article or a Twitter thread, but something that requires sustained attention over hours or days. Your mind has to do several things at once. It has to hold the narrative thread while tracking character development. It has to remember what happened fifty pages ago and connect it to what's happening now. It has to infer what's not explicitly stated. It has to pause when something resonates, return to passages that confused you, let images form in your imagination.

This is cognitive work. It's training. Every time you sit with a book for an hour, you're strengthening the mental muscles that allow for depth. You're practicing the ability to stay with something difficult, to tolerate confusion until clarity arrives, to resist the urge to skim when the pace slows. You're learning that not everything yields its meaning immediately—that some things require patience, attention, and the willingness to sit in uncertainty.

Now consider what happens when you scroll. Your attention lands on a headline, absorbs a fragment of information, moves on. Fifteen seconds later, you've forgotten what you read. Your mind never has to hold anything—it just has to react. There's no narrative to track, no complexity to navigate, no ambiguity to sit with. Everything is designed for instant comprehension and instant forgetting. Scroll, absorb, react, move on. Scroll, absorb, react, move on.

This isn't neutral. It's training too—but it's training in the opposite direction. It's training your mind to skim rather than dwell, to react rather than reflect, to move on before anything has time to take root. Do this for hours a day, every day, for years, and you've fundamentally reshaped your cognitive capacity. The muscle of sustained attention atrophies. The ability to sit with difficulty weakens.

The tolerance for boredom—which is really just the space between stimulus and insight—disappears entirely.

The person who can't read a book anymore isn't lazy. They've been trained out of the capacity. Their attention span has been shortened through thousands of micro-interactions that rewarded speed and punished depth. And once that capacity is gone, it's hard to recover. Trying to read feels frustrating, exhausting, pointless. The mind keeps wandering. The urge to check the phone becomes overwhelming. The book sits unfinished because the person no longer has the attentional infrastructure to complete it.

This is why the recovery of interior life requires the recovery of reading—not as a hobby or leisure activity, but as a practice. Reading is to attention what exercise is to the body. It's how you build the capacity for sustained focus. It's how you learn to think in paragraphs instead of sentences, in chapters instead of fragments. It's how you develop the ability to follow an argument through its complexities rather than just reacting to its conclusion.

And it's not just about intellectual development. Reading fiction, in particular, builds empathy by letting you inhabit another person's interior world for hours at a time. You see through their eyes, feel what they feel, understand motivations that aren't your own. This is the opposite of what social media does—which flattens everyone into caricature and rewards you for dismissing people you disagree with. A person who reads novels is less likely to reduce others to their worst moment or their most inflammatory statement, because they've practiced seeing human complexity.

The collapse of reading isn't just about books. It's about the collapse of the mental capacity that makes depth possible. A culture that doesn't read is a culture that can't think, can't sustain attention, can't hold complexity. And a person who doesn't read becomes a shallower version of who they could have been—not because reading makes you superior, but because it develops capacities that nothing else develops quite the same way.

People now communicate in fragments. Texts instead of letters. Tweets instead of essays. Emojis instead of sentences. This isn't just about technology—it's about the collapse of the mental infrastructure that makes complex communication possible. You can't write a thoughtful paragraph if you can't hold a thought for more than thirty seconds. You can't follow a complex argument if your mind keeps drifting. You can't say what you mean if you've never spent time figuring out what you mean.

The irony is that people feel more connected than ever while being more isolated than ever. They're in constant contact—texting, posting, commenting—but the contact is shallow. Real connection requires presence, and presence requires attention. When two people sit together but both are checking their phones, they're not together. When someone tells you something important and you're half-listening while mentally composing a reply, you're not present. Connection isn't about proximity or frequency of contact. It's about the quality of attention you bring to another person.

Consider what happens at a family dinner when everyone brings their phone to the table. The conversation starts, but it's interrupted every few minutes by someone checking a notification, responding to a text, scrolling through something. The eight-year-old is telling a story about school, but Dad glances at his email mid-sentence. Mom is physically present but mentally elsewhere, trying to remember if she responded to that work message. The teenager isn't even pretending to listen—she's texting under the table.

What's actually happening here? Not a meal. Not a conversation. Not connection. What's happening is the performance of family life while everyone's attention is elsewhere. The child learns that what they're saying isn't important enough to command full attention. The spouse learns that work takes precedence over presence. Everyone learns that relationships are something you fit in around more important things—or that relationships don't require your full self, just your physical proximity.

The cost accumulates slowly. Marriages erode not through dramatic betrayals but through thousands of small moments of inattention. One spouse tries to share something that matters, but the other is half-present, giving distracted "uh-huhs" while scrolling. The conversation dies. The spouse stops trying. Over months and years, they learn that their partner isn't really available—not because they're gone, but because they're never fully there. Intimacy requires presence. Without it, people become roommates who share a house but not a life.

The same pattern destroys friendships. You meet for coffee, but your friend keeps checking their phone. They're apologetic about it—work is crazy, family is demanding—but the result is the same. You're talking, but they're not listening. Not really. They hear your words but miss everything underneath: the hesitation that signals uncertainty, the slight change in tone that reveals hurt, the pause that invites them to ask a deeper question. Those cues require attention. Without attention, conversation becomes an exchange of information rather than a meeting of persons.

Children are particularly vulnerable to this. A young child doesn't understand that Dad is distracted by something important. They just know that Dad isn't present. They'll keep trying for a while—"Dad, watch this! Dad, look!"—but eventually they stop. They learn that adults aren't fully available, that their presence doesn't command attention, that they're less interesting than whatever is on the screen. This doesn't produce immediate harm. It produces children who grow up feeling slightly invisible, slightly unimportant, slightly unsure whether they matter enough to hold anyone's full attention.

What makes this particularly insidious is that everyone involved can be well-intentioned. The distracted parent loves his child. The distracted spouse loves her partner. The distracted friend values the friendship. But love and attention aren't the same thing. Love is a commitment. Attention is a practice. And you can be committed to someone while systematically failing to give them the one thing that makes the commitment real: your presence.

The recovery here is simple but not easy: put the phone away. Not on the table face-down. Not in your pocket where you can feel it vibrate. In another room. Out of reach. Create spaces—meals, conversations, bedtime—where attention is protected, where the people in front of you know they have you completely. Leave the work phone—I mentioned my personal boundary in this regard at the beginning of the chapter—and take the spouse and children to a movie without it. This feels drastic at first. What if something urgent happens? What if you miss something important? But those fears are almost always unfounded. The urgent things can wait an hour. And the important thing—the relationship in front of you—is happening right now, while you're distracted.

The hardest part is recognizing how much you've normalized distraction. Most people don't think they're inattentive. They think they're managing multiple priorities—multitasking. But from the outside—from the child's perspective, the spouse's perspective, the friend's perspective—it looks like absence. And over time, absence becomes the defining feature of the relationship. Not absence of the body, but absence of the self. You're there, but you're not there. And eventually, people stop expecting you to be.

This is what distraction does to language too. When attention goes, words go with it. Not the words themselves—we still speak plenty of them—but their weight. A person who is half-present gives half-words: reassurances without conviction, agreements without commitment, apologies without repair. Language spoken without attention is language that doesn't mean what it says. And the people on the receiving end know it. They hear the words and sense the absence behind them. Over time, they stop listening—not because the words have stopped, but because the words have stopped carrying anything worth listening to.

The recovery of attention begins with the willingness to be bored. Boredom has become the enemy in modern life, something to be eliminated as quickly as possible. But boredom is actually a gift. It's the signal that your mind is ready to wander, to explore, to make connections it couldn't make while distracted. The best ideas don't come from scrolling—they come from staring at the ceiling, walking without a destination, sitting on a porch doing nothing. Boredom is the doorway to creativity, but only if you don't slam it shut by reaching for your phone.

Recovering interior life also requires recovering solitude. Not loneliness—solitude. The ability to be alone without feeling like something's wrong. Solitude is where you encounter yourself, where you learn who you are when no one else is watching, where you develop the internal resources that make you capable of being good company for others. A person who can't be alone becomes dependent on others for their sense of self. A person comfortable in solitude becomes self-possessed, which is a different thing entirely from selfish.

It also requires recovering the habit of reflection. This doesn't mean constant self-analysis. It just means spending a few minutes each day reviewing what happened, how you responded, what you learned, what you want to do differently. Most people never do this. They move from one day to the next without ever pausing to process. The days accumulate but don't cohere into a story. Reflection is what turns experience into wisdom.

And it requires defending your attention as a finite resource. You can't pay attention to everything. You must choose. And what you choose becomes what you are. If you spend your attention on outrage, you'll become perpetually angry. If you spend it on gossip, you'll become shallow. If you spend it on beauty, truth, and goodness, you'll become capable of recognizing them. Attention is the most valuable thing you possess, and the modern world is designed to steal it from you. Recovering it is an act of resistance.

Some practical steps help. Put the phone in another room. Turn off notifications. Create spaces in the day that are protected from interruption. Walk without listening to anything. Sit in silence for ten minutes. Write by hand. Spend your lunch break reading books not related to work instead of technical articles. Have conversations without checking the time. These aren't revolutionary acts, but they create the conditions for depth to return.

The recovery of attention won't happen quickly. The habits that destroyed it took years to form. The habits that restore it will take time too. But the payoff is enormous. A person who has learned to sustain attention is less anxious, less reactive, less dependent on external validation. They know themselves. They can sit with difficulty without being destroyed by it. They can think through complexity without needing someone else to tell them what to believe. They can be alone without being lonely and present with others without losing themselves.

They become, in the old sense, self-possessed. Not arrogant or isolated, but grounded. The kind of person who can listen, who can think, who can speak from depth rather than reflex. The kind of person whose words carry weight because there's substance behind them.

William James was right. We really do become what we pay attention to. And in an age designed to fragment attention into a thousand shallow streams, recovering depth is one of the most important forms of resistance available.

Not because depth makes you superior to others, but because it makes you capable of living fully. It restores the capacity for wonder, for insight, for connection, for meaning. It lets you inhabit your own life instead of merely passing through it.

The world will keep being loud. The devices will keep demanding attention. The earbuds will keep blocking out people and activities around you. The culture will keep rewarding speed over reflection, motion over stillness, reaction over thought.

But the interior life can still be recovered. One moment of attention at a time. One hour of solitude at a time. One choice to be present instead of distracted. And when enough people recover it—when enough people remember what it feels like to dwell rather than skim, to think rather than react, to be rather than perform—the language will begin to deepen again.

The words we once knew will be waiting, sharp and ready, exactly where we left them.

THIRTEEN

LOVE, LISTENING, AND HOME

Love, listening, and *home* aren't separate words that happen to appear together—they're three sides of a triangle, three legs of a stool. You can't love well without listening. You can't listen deeply without love. And home is simply the place where both are practiced daily, in the presence of people who see you at your worst and choose to stay anyway.

These three also depend entirely on what the previous chapter examined: attention. Without the capacity to sustain attention, love becomes sentiment—a feeling you experience rather than a discipline you practice. Without attention, listening becomes waiting for your turn to speak. Without attention, home becomes a building where people sleep under the same roof but remain strangers to each other.

So this chapter isn't about three degraded words—it's about three *interwoven practices* that have thinned together, all for the same reason: we've lost the capacity for the kind of sustained, generous attention that makes any of them possible.

Most of what we say each day is not chosen—it's habitual. The tone we use with a spouse. The patience (or impatience) we extend to a child. The way we respond when someone interrupts us. These patterns form so gradually that we don't notice them becoming fixed. But over time, they create the emotional weather of a home, the atmosphere in which relationships either flourish or wither.

Language shapes love more than most people realize. Not the grand declarations—though those matter—but the daily accumulation of ordinary words. The greeting when someone walks through the door. The tone in which a request is made. The words chosen in a moment of frustration. These small exchanges, repeated hundreds of times, become the texture of a relationship. They signal safety or tension, warmth or distance, presence or distraction.

A marriage can survive conflict. It can survive hardship. But it struggles to survive contempt, and contempt often enters not through dramatic confrontations but through the small erosions of daily speech. The sarcastic remark. The dismissive tone. The interruption that signals "what you're saying doesn't matter." The habit of correcting rather than listening. These aren't usually conscious cruelties—they're patterns formed in moments of stress or fatigue—but they compound. And once established, they're hard to reverse.

The opposite is also true. A relationship strengthens through the habits of generous speech. The specific thank-you that names what was noticed. The question that invites the other person to say what they're actually thinking. The willingness to apologize without defending. The patience to listen past the words to what's beneath them. These, too, are habits. And like all habits, they're formed through repetition.

Love, in its mature form, is not primarily a feeling. Feelings come and go—they rise with circumstance and fade with exhaustion. Love is a discipline, practiced daily in the choices we make about how we speak. The person who loves well learns to choose words that build rather than diminish, that create space rather than close it, that honor rather than wound.

This doesn't mean false cheerfulness or the suppression of honest disagreement. It means speaking with intention. It means pausing long enough before responding to ask: Will this help or harm? Will this bring us closer or push us apart? Am I speaking from frustration or from care? These questions don't eliminate conflict, but they prevent careless speech from creating unnecessary damage.

The home is where unguarded language lives. It's where people speak without the polish they use in public, where fatigue shows, where patience runs thin. This is natural—no one can maintain a public persona at home. But it also means that home is where people are most vulnerable to being wounded by the words of those they love.

Children, especially, absorb the tone of a household long before they understand the content of conversations. They learn what anger sounds like, what affection sounds like, what tension sounds like. They learn whether apologies are possible, whether mistakes are forgiven, whether people repair what they've broken. The language of a home becomes the template for how they'll speak in their own relationships decades later.

A sharp word spoken to a child in frustration can echo for years. Not because the child holds a grudge, but because children interpret adult speech as truth about themselves. "You're so careless" becomes "I am careless." "Why can't you ever listen?" becomes "I am bad at listening." The words stick, even when the parent has long forgotten saying them. This doesn't mean parents must be perfect—perfection is impossible and wouldn't be useful even if it were possible. But it means words spoken at home carry more weight than words spoken anywhere else.

The same is true in marriage. A spouse hears not only what you say but what your tone implies. A dismissive tone says "you don't matter." An impatient tone says "you're a burden." A distracted tone says "something else is more important than you." These messages are often unintended—delivered in moments of stress, not malice—but they land nonetheless. And over time, they shape how safe a person feels in the relationship.

Repair is possible, but it requires more than time. It requires acknowledgment. The willingness to say, "I was harsh earlier. I'm sorry. That wasn't fair." These small acts of repair prevent resentment from accumulating. They signal that the relationship matters more than being right, that dignity matters more than pride.

But not all apologies repair. Some actually make things worse.

The non-apology is easy to spot once you know what to look for. "I'm sorry you felt that way." "I'm sorry if I hurt you." "I'm sorry, but you also..." These aren't apologies—they're defenses disguised as apologies. They shift responsibility from the speaker to the listener, suggesting that the problem isn't what was said but how it was received. The hurt person is left feeling dismissed twice: once by the original harm, and again by the refusal to acknowledge it.

Real repair requires three elements: acknowledgment of what you actually did, recognition of its impact, and commitment to change. "I was dismissive when you were trying to tell me about your day. That was disrespectful, and it probably made you feel like I don't care about what matters to you. I'm going to work on being more present when we talk." This is harder than "I'm sorry if I upset you" because it requires looking directly at your own behavior instead of deflecting to the other person's reaction.

The other common failure is the apology that's technically accurate but emotionally hollow. The words are right, but the tone conveys annoyance or impatience—"Fine, I'm sorry, okay?"—as though the apology is a burden being extracted under protest. This doesn't repair anything. It just adds another layer of injury: not only were you hurt, but now you're being treated as unreasonable for wanting acknowledgment.

Children learn about repair by watching how adults handle it. The parent who apologizes genuinely teaches the child that mistakes don't define you—how you respond to them does. The parent who never apologizes teaches the child that admitting fault is weakness, that authority means never being wrong, that relationships are about power rather than mutuality. And the parent who offers hollow apologies teaches the child that words don't have to mean anything, that you can say "I'm sorry" while communicating "I'm not really sorry at all."

Genuine repair also doesn't demand immediate forgiveness. It allows the hurt person time to process. "I understand if you're still upset. I don't expect this to be fixed immediately. I just wanted you to know that I see what I did and I'm sorry." This respects the reality that some words do damage that takes time to heal. Rushing to reconciliation—"I said I was sorry, why are you still upset?"—compounds the injury by suggesting that the hurt person's feelings are inconvenient or unreasonable.

Over time, a pattern of genuine repair builds something that nothing else can build: the confidence that when things go wrong, they can be made right. Not perfectly—the original harm still happened—but sufficiently. The relationship can survive conflict because both people know that mistakes will be acknowledged, that repair will be attempted, that the relationship is more important than individual pride.

This confidence is what makes intimacy possible. You can be vulnerable with someone when you know that if they wound you—even accidentally—they'll care enough to repair it. But if repair is impossible, if apologies are always hollow or defensive, vulnerability becomes too dangerous. You learn to protect yourself, to keep parts of yourself hidden, to never fully trust that the other person will handle you carefully.

The homes where repair happens regularly are the homes where people can be honest. They can risk saying something difficult because they know that if it comes out wrong, repair is possible. They can be themselves—imperfect, sometimes clumsy, occasionally hurtful—because they trust that mistakes don't end things. The relationship is stronger than any single failure.

The homes where repair never happens are the homes where people walk on eggshells, where honesty feels dangerous, where resentment accumulates in silence because there's no path back from conflict to connection.

Repair isn't a sign that something's wrong with the relationship. It's a sign that something's right—that both people value the relationship enough to do the hard work of acknowledging harm and making it right.

Listening is its own form of love. Not the passive kind of listening where you wait for your turn to speak, but the active kind where you're genuinely trying to understand what the other person means. This is harder than it sounds. Most people, when listening, are mentally preparing their response, finding the flaw in the other person's reasoning, or waiting for a pause so they can redirect the conversation. Real listening requires setting all of that aside and being present to what's actually being said.

Real listening also requires humility. It requires the possibility that you might learn something, that your understanding might be incomplete, that the other person's perspective might reveal something you hadn't considered. Without that humility, listening becomes performance—an act you go through while waiting to assert what you already believe.

People often underestimate how much they long to be heard. Not agreed with, not fixed, not advised—just heard. The experience of feeling truly listened to is so rare that when it happens, it can shift an entire relationship. Marriages improve. Friendships deepen. Parent-child relationships stabilize. All because someone finally felt that their words mattered enough for another person to really attend to them.

Listening is also a discipline that improves with practice. You learn to hear not just the surface complaint but the underlying need. You learn to recognize when someone needs advice and when they need companionship. You learn to sit with someone's pain without rushing to fix it, to sit with someone's joy without redirecting the conversation toward yourself. These are skills, not instincts. They develop slowly, through the willingness to pay attention.

But listening is only half of the equation. Speaking matters too—not just what you say, but how you invite the other person into the conversation. Questions matter. Not interrogations, but genuine curiosity. "What are you thinking about?" "How did that feel for you?" "What do you need right now?" These questions signal that the other person's interior world matters, that you're interested in more than just the surface.

The quality of conversation in a home determines much of its emotional temperature. Homes where people talk past each other become lonely places, even when multiple people are present. Homes where people interrupt constantly become chaotic. Homes where difficult topics are avoided become brittle—tension accumulates beneath a surface of false calm. But homes where people speak honestly, listen generously, and repair mistakes become places where people want to be.

The language we bring home reveals who we're becoming. Public language is curated—we edit, we filter, we choose words that present us well. But at home, the unguarded version appears. The tone that emerges when we're tired. The words that come out when we're frustrated. The amount of patience we extend when no one else is watching. These are the truest indicators of character because they're the least performed.

One of the hardest truths to face is how quickly kind speech can turn cruel when anger takes over. I know this because I've done it. The sharp remark that's designed to sting. The sarcastic tone that dismisses rather than engages. The raising of voice that's meant to force attention rather than invite it. In those moments, I'm not speaking from my best self—I'm speaking from the part that wants to wound because I feel wounded. And the damage those words do doesn't disappear when the anger passes. They lodge in memory. They change how safe the other person feels. They make the next conversation harder because trust has been chipped away.

The worst part is how automatic it becomes. Anger speaks before thought does. The harsh words are out before you've decided to say them. And by the time you realize what you've done, the other person is already hurt. You can apologize—and you should—but apology doesn't erase what was said. It only begins repair.

This is why the language of home matters so much. It's where we're most ourselves, and where the people we love most encounter that self without the protective layers we maintain elsewhere. If the unguarded self is harsh, impatient, or dismissive, that's what the people closest to us experience. If the unguarded self is gentle, attentive, and kind, that's what they receive.

This doesn't mean we need to be saints at home. It means we need to be honest about the patterns we're creating and willing to change them when they're causing harm. A person who snaps at their spouse every evening might justify it as stress from work, but the spouse experiences it as rejection. A parent who never has time to really listen might believe they're providing by working hard, but the child experiences it as absence.

The gap between intention and impact is where most relational damage occurs. And closing that gap requires paying attention to how our words actually land, not just how we meant them.

Consider the husband who justifies his harsh tone by saying, "I'm just being honest. You wanted me to be honest, didn't you?" He means this as a defense: his intentions were good, so the impact shouldn't matter. But honesty without kindness isn't honesty—it's cruelty wearing a virtue's name. You can tell the truth in ways that honor the other person or in ways that wound them. The choice of how to speak reveals whether you actually care about the impact your words have.

Or consider the parent who's never available for conversation, always working, always busy, always stressed. When the child finally says, "You're never around," the parent responds: "I'm working to provide for this family. Everything I do is for you." And that might be true—the parent's intention is to provide. But the child's experience is abandonment. The parent meant well. The child still grew up feeling unimportant. Both things are true. And the parent who can't see past their good intentions to acknowledge the child's actual experience will never close the gap.

The problem is that we judge ourselves by our intentions and others by their impact. When I speak harshly, I know I didn't mean to hurt anyone—I was just tired, just stressed, just frustrated. But when someone speaks harshly to me, I don't have access to their interior state. I only have the words that landed on me. And those words hurt, regardless of what the speaker intended.

This asymmetry makes it easy to excuse our own behavior while holding others accountable for theirs. "I didn't mean it that way" becomes a complete defense when we're the speaker. But when we're on the receiving end, "I didn't mean it that way" sounds like a dodge, an excuse, a refusal to take responsibility.

Closing the gap requires developing the habit of asking, "How did that sound to her?" instead of defending with "That's not what I meant." It requires accepting that your impact matters more than your intention—not because intentions are irrelevant, but because the person in front of you is experiencing the impact, not the intention. They're living with the words you actually said, not the words you wish you'd said or the meaning you hoped they'd hear.

This is especially important in the relationships that matter most. A colleague at work might give you the benefit of the doubt. They'll interpret your words charitably because the relationship isn't deep enough for words to cut very far. But a spouse, a child, a close friend—they're vulnerable in ways that acquaintances aren't. Your words reach deeper. The potential for harm is greater. And that means the responsibility to pay attention to impact is greater too.

Some people resist this. They argue that constantly monitoring impact is exhausting, that it means walking on eggshells, that it prevents honest communication. But that's a misunderstanding. Paying attention to impact doesn't mean lying or suppressing truth. It means choosing words carefully. It means pausing before speaking to ask: Is this true? Is this kind? Is this necessary? Will this help or harm?

These questions don't eliminate conflict. They prevent careless speech from creating unnecessary conflict. There's a difference between the conflict that comes from genuine disagreement and the conflict that comes from speaking without thought. The first kind can be productive. The second kind just damages people.

The person who learns to attend to impact without abandoning honesty becomes someone people can trust. They don't wound carelessly. They don't hide behind "I was just being honest" when they've been harsh. They don't defend their intentions when they've caused harm. They simply say: "I see that hurt you. I'm sorry. Let me try again."

That willingness—to see past your own intentions to the other person's experience, to own the impact you've had even when you didn't mean to cause it, to try again with more care—is what transforms relationships from fragile to resilient.

Suffering also changes how we speak if we let it. Grief, loss, disappointment—these experiences can make people bitter or they can make people gentle. The difference often comes down to whether a person is willing to let suffering teach them. Those who allow it often become better listeners, more patient speakers, less quick to judge. They've been broken enough to know that harshness doesn't help, that everyone is carrying more than they show, that gentleness is a form of strength.

When someone who has suffered deeply speaks, their words often carry a different quality—less performance, more presence. They're not trying to impress or dominate. They've learned that life is too short and too fragile for unnecessary cruelty. This doesn't make them weak. It makes them trustworthy.

The goal of all this—the careful speech, the generous listening, the willingness to repair—is not harmony for its own sake. Harmony is nice, but it's not the deepest good. The goal is intimacy. The experience of being known and still loved. The security of knowing you can speak truthfully without being abandoned. The trust that comes from years of small fidelities—promises kept, apologies offered, attention given.

Intimacy can't be manufactured. It grows slowly, through the accumulation of moments where someone chose connection over convenience, honesty over avoidance, repair over defensiveness. Language is the medium in which intimacy forms. Not grand speeches, but the daily discipline of speaking and listening in ways that honor the other person's humanity.

The language of home is also where we become the people our words assume we are. If you speak with patience, you become more patient. If you speak with generosity, you become more generous. If you apologize when you're wrong, you become someone capable of growth. Character and speech shape each other. Over time, the gap between who you are and who you speak like you are closes—not because you've perfected your performance, but because you've allowed your words to form you.

This is why recovering meaningful language has to include recovering the language of home. All the public virtues—truth, responsibility, courage, reverence—are tested first in private. A person who can't speak truthfully to their spouse won't speak truthfully in public. A person who won't apologize to their child won't apologize to a colleague. A person who doesn't listen at home won't listen anywhere.

The home is the laboratory where language either deepens or thins. And what happens there ripples outward into every other area of life.

So the work of restoring language begins, as all real work does, in the places no one else sees. In the tone you use when you're tired. In the patience you extend when you're frustrated. In the apology you offer when you're wrong. In the attention you give when someone needs to be heard.

These are small acts, easily overlooked, rarely celebrated. But they're also the acts that build lives worth living and relationships worth keeping. Because in the end, love is not what we feel. It's what we do with our words, day after day, when no one else is watching.

And the people we love know this, even when we forget it.

Fourteen

EXCELLENCE

We are what we repeatedly do. Excellence, then, is not an act, but a habit.
—Aristotle

Excellence has become a suspicious word. It sounds elitist, exclusionary, judgmental. In a culture committed to equality of outcome, to making everyone feel valued regardless of performance, to celebrating participation over achievement, excellence feels like a relic of a harsher time when people were ranked, sorted, and told that some were better than others.

But excellence never meant some people are worth more than others. It meant some work is better than other work, some performances are stronger than other performances, some achievements represent higher skill than others. Excellence was about the work, not the person. It was about what you did, not who you were. And the possibility of excellence—the recognition that better exists and is worth striving for—is what made improvement possible.

That possibility is disappearing. We're told that standards are oppressive, that judgment is harmful, that distinguishing between excellent and adequate is a form of violence. We're moving toward a world where everyone gets a trophy, every student gets an A, every employee gets a raise, and no one is ever told that their work isn't good enough—because good enough has become whatever you produced.

This sounds compassionate. It sounds like we're protecting people from the pain of failure, from the shame of inadequacy, from the trauma of being judged. But we're not protecting them. We're disabling them. Because without the possibility of excellence, there's no reason to improve. Without honest assessment, there's no way to know what needs work. Without standards, there's no way to measure progress.

Excellence used to mean the best possible version of something—not perfection, but the highest standard achievable given the constraints. A piece of furniture could be excellent even if it wasn't flawless because excellence meant it was crafted with skill, attention, and care. A meal could be excellent even if it wasn't innovative because excellence meant it was prepared thoughtfully and executed well. A student's work could be excellent even if it wasn't groundbreaking because excellence meant they'd pushed themselves to understand deeply and express clearly.

The standard wasn't arbitrary. It emerged from the accumulated wisdom of people who'd done the thing before, who knew what mastery looked like, who could distinguish between work that showed understanding and work that showed confusion. Excellence was the target you aimed for—rarely hit perfectly, but always worth pursuing.

That standard has been eroded by several cultural shifts that each seemed reasonable but collectively destroyed the concept.

First, the self-esteem movement decided that feeling good about yourself was more important than actually being good at things. Children were praised constantly, not for genuine achievement but just for trying, or for showing up, or for existing. The idea was that building confidence would lead to competence. But it worked backward. Confidence without competence is just delusion. And when children who'd been praised for everything encountered real standards, they broke—not because the standards were too high, but because they'd never learned to meet any standard at all.

Second, the equity movement conflated equal dignity with equal outcomes. The recognition that all people have inherent worth—regardless of ability, achievement, or status—is true and important. But that truth got twisted into the idea that all outcomes should be equal, that any difference in achievement is evidence of injustice, that standards themselves are oppressive because they produce unequal results. This confusion is catastrophic. You can believe in equal human dignity while recognizing that some people write better than others, calculate better than others, play saxophone better than others. Excellence isn't about worth—it's about performance. And performance varies.

Third, the participation trophy culture removed the distinction between trying and succeeding. Everyone who showed up got recognized, regardless of how they performed. The intent was to prevent children from feeling like failures. But the effect was to teach them that effort and outcome are the same thing, that showing up is sufficient, that you don't actually have to be good at something to be treated as though you are. This produces adults who can't handle honest feedback, who experience any criticism as a personal attack, who've never developed the resilience that comes from failing, adjusting, and improving.

Fourth, grade inflation made it nearly impossible to distinguish excellent work from adequate work. At many universities, the average grade is now an A-minus. This doesn't mean students are learning more—it means grades no longer mean anything. When everyone gets high marks regardless of performance, grades stop being useful information about competence. And without that information, students can't identify where they need to improve, and employers can't identify who actually knows what they're doing.

The result is a culture that can't pursue excellence because it can't admit that excellence exists. We've replaced it with affirmation—everyone is doing great, everyone is special, everyone deserves recognition. And in the short term, this feels kind. But in the long term, it's cruel. Because reality doesn't grade on a curve. Reality has standards. And people who've never been held to standards will eventually encounter reality—and won't have the tools to meet it.

Here's what the loss of excellence looks like in practice.

A high school teacher assigns an essay. Half the students turn in work that's poorly reasoned, badly organized, and full of grammatical errors. The teacher knows these essays aren't good. But giving them the grades they deserve—D's and F's—will upset the students, anger the parents, and create problems with admin-istrators who are judged on pass rates. So the teacher gives them B-minuses and

C-pluses, with encouraging comments about improvement. The students learn nothing except that mediocre work is acceptable. They don't improve because they don't know they need to.

Or consider a workplace where performance reviews have become entirely positive. Everyone is "meeting expectations" or "exceeding expectations." No one is ever told their work is substandard because that might hurt feelings or create legal liability. But this means people who are underperforming never know it, never get the feedback they need to improve, and eventually get fired—not because anyone told them what was wrong, but because the gap between their performance and what's needed became impossible to ignore. They're shocked because they thought they were doing fine. No one had been honest with them.

Or think about college admissions, where standards have been lowered or eliminated in the name of equity. Students who aren't prepared for college-level work are admitted anyway. They struggle, not because they lack ability, but because they lack preparation. Many drop out. Those who persist often graduate without having learned what college was supposed to teach them. And the degree they earn—the credential that's supposed to signal competence—no longer signals anything, because institutions stopped holding students to standards.

In each case, the intention was compassion. But the effect is harm. Because people need honest feedback. They need to know when their work isn't good enough. They need standards to aim for. Without these, they can't improve, can't develop competence, can't become truly capable.

I work in a world where excellence is not optional. When an air conditioning systems serves operating rooms, the systems must perform as designed—not approximately, not close enough, not "good enough given the circumstances." The surgeons working on the other end of those systems don't grade on a curve. The patients don't give partial credit. Excellence in that environment isn't a standard imposed arbitrarily from the outside. It's what the work requires. And everyone involved understands that the distance between excellent and adequate can be measured in outcomes that nobody wants to talk about.

This sounds extreme because it is extreme. Most people don't work in environments where the stakes are that immediate. But the principle is the same everywhere: standards exist because the work requires them, not because someone wants to make you feel inadequate. The student whose poorly argued paper gets a B-minus instead of a D will eventually enter a world where her work will be evaluated against what it actually accomplishes, not against what she wished she'd produced. When that happens, she'll find herself unprepared—not because she wasn't capable, but because no one ever told her she needed to be better.

Excellence also depends on honest judgment—the willingness to say "this is better than that." And honest judgment has become nearly impossible. We've been taught that all such judgments are subjective, that quality is just personal preference, that saying one thing is better than another is arrogant or oppressive.

But this is nonsense. Some writing is clearer than other writing. Some arguments are stronger than other arguments. Some craftsmanship is more skilled than other craftsmanship. These aren't just opinions—they're assessments based on criteria that have been refined over time by people who know what they're doing. You can disagree about the criteria, but you can't pretend criteria don't exist.

A Bach fugue is more complex and technically sophisticated than "Twinkle, Twinkle, Little Star." That's not a value judgment about which one is more meaningful to you personally—it's an objective assessment of musical complexity. Both can be enjoyed. Both can be appropriate in different contexts. But pretending they're equally excellent as musical compositions is just dishonest.

The same applies everywhere. A carefully researched, well-argued essay is better than one that's sloppy and poorly reasoned. A house built to code by skilled craftsmen is better than one slapped together by amateurs. A surgeon who's performed a procedure a thousand times is better at it than one who's done it twice. These judgments aren't elitist—they're just accurate.

Excellence matters because it represents the highest human capabilities. It shows what's possible when skill, effort, and discipline converge. It sets a standard that others can aim for. It demonstrates that some things are worth doing well, that the difference between adequate and excellent is real, and that the pursuit of excellence produces results that benefit everyone.

The alternative—a world where excellence is dismissed as elitist, where standards are abolished as oppressive, where everyone is told they're doing great regardless of how they're actually doing—is a world where nothing improves. Where mediocrity becomes the ceiling because there's no reason to aim higher. Where people who could become excellent never do because no one ever told them they could be better.

So how do we recover excellence?

First, we separate excellence from worth. A person's value doesn't depend on their achievements. You can be a person of great worth while producing mediocre work. And you can be a person of questionable character and worth while producing excellent work. Worth and excellence operate in different domains. Confusing them—treating criticism of work as criticism of person—is what makes honest assessment feel like personal attack.

Second, we must recover honest feedback. This means praising what's genuinely good and identifying what needs improvement. Not cruelly, not dismissively, but honestly. "This essay has strong ideas but the organization needs work" is more helpful than "Great job!" when the organization actually does need work. Honest feedback is an act of respect—it treats the person as capable of improvement rather than as too fragile to handle criticism.

Third, we need to restore standards. Not arbitrary or capricious standards, but legitimate ones based on what competence in a field actually requires. In writing, that means clarity, organization, evidence, and grammar. In mathematics, that means correct reasoning and accurate calculation. In craftsmanship, that means precision, durability, and attention to detail. These standards aren't oppressive—they're the accumulated wisdom of people who know what they're doing.

Fourth, we must accept that pursuit of excellence requires failure. You don't get excellent by succeeding at easy things. You get excellent by attempting hard things, failing, learning from the failure, and trying again. A culture that protects people from failure protects them from excellence. Because excellence is always on the other side of repeated failure.

Fifth, we need to recognize that excellence is achievable at any level. You don't have to be the best in the world to pursue excellence. You just have to aim for the best you're capable of. The carpenter who makes furniture with care and skill is pursuing excellence, even if they're not a famous artisan. The teacher who prepares thoughtfully and explains clearly is pursuing excellence, even if they're not a celebrity educator. Excellence isn't about comparison to others—it's about the standard you hold yourself to.

Sixth, stop treating judgment as violence. Saying "this work doesn't meet the standard" isn't an attack. It's information. Information someone needs if they're going to improve. The student who submits a poorly written essay needs to know it's poorly written. The employee whose work is substandard needs to know it's substandard. Withholding that information doesn't protect them—it ensures they'll never get better.

Finally, we must remember that excellence is its own reward. The satisfaction of doing something well, of pushing yourself to your limits, of producing work that meets a high standard—that matters independently of external recognition. People who've experienced excellence know this. They know the difference between work they're proud of and work they're not. And that internal standard is often more demanding than any external one.

Excellence also has a communal dimension. When a culture values excellence, it creates environments where excellent work is recognized, rewarded, and emulated. People see what's possible and are inspired to pursue it themselves. Standards rise because everyone is pushing each other higher. Mediocrity becomes unacceptable not because people are cruel, but because excellence is expected and achievable.

But when a culture abandons excellence—when it treats all work as equally good, when it refuses to judge, when it praises effort regardless of outcome—it creates a race to the bottom. Why work hard when adequate effort gets the same recognition? Why pursue mastery when competence is treated as optional? Why develop skill when skill isn't rewarded?

The loss of excellence produces a particular kind of poverty: not material poverty, but poverty of achievement. A world where nothing is excellent because excellence has been abolished as a concept. Where people go through the motions without ever pushing themselves to see what they're capable of. Where potential remains unrealized because no one ever challenged anyone to realize it.

This poverty harms everyone, but it especially harms the people it claims to protect. The student who's never held to a standard never learns to meet one. The employee who's never given honest feedback never improves. The artist who's told everything they produce is wonderful never develops genuine skill. They're trapped in mediocrity by the very affirmation that was supposed to help them.

Real compassion tells the truth. Real compassion says "you can do better" and then shows you how. Real compassion holds you to a standard because it believes you're capable of meeting it. That might feel harsh in the moment, but it's actually the deepest form of respect. It says: I believe in your potential enough to push you toward it.

Excellence is how human beings become fully themselves. Not by being perfect, not by being better than others, but by developing their capabilities as fully as possible. By learning to do things well. By discovering what they're capable of when they push past what's comfortable. By developing mastery in some domain, however small.

That possibility—the possibility of excellence—is what makes human life more than just existence. It's what turns work into craft, effort into achievement, potential into reality. And when we lose it, we lose something essential about what it means to be human.

The world still needs people who can do things excellently. Who can write clearly, think rigorously, build carefully, teach effectively, create beautifully. Who hold themselves to standards and produce work that meets them. Who know the difference between good enough and actually good, and who care about that difference.

Excellence isn't elitism. It's not about being better than other people. It's about being better than you were yesterday, about doing work that matters, about holding yourself to a standard even when no one else is watching.

Excellence is the refusal to settle for adequate when excellent is possible. And it's one of the few things that can't be taken from you—only abandoned. The culture may have given up on excellence. It may have decided that standards are oppressive, that judgment is harmful, that everyone deserves recognition regardless of performance.

But individuals don't have to accept that. You can still pursue excellence in your own work. You can still hold yourself to standards. You can still care about doing things well, even when the culture has stopped noticing the difference between well and barely.

And when enough people do that—when enough people refuse to settle, refuse to accept mediocrity, refuse to pretend that adequate is the same as excellent—the culture begins to shift. Not because of grand pronouncements or institutional changes, but because excellence, once seen, is compelling. It reminds people what's possible. It shows what happens when care, skill, and discipline converge.

That's what we're passing forward: not perfect work, but excellent work. Not flawless performance, but genuine mastery. Not the pretense that everyone is equally good at everything, but the truth that everyone is capable of excellence in something—if they're willing to pursue it.

Stewardship requires excellence. You can't maintain what you've inherited if you don't know how to do things well. You can't pass forward something better than you received if you've settled for adequate. Excellence is what allows each generation to hand forward something worth having.

And it begins with the simple recognition that better exists, that it's worth pursuing, and that the difference between adequate and excellent matters—not because excellent people are worth more, but because excellent work serves the world better.

That's what the next generation deserves: not empty praise, not participation trophies, not the lie that everything they do is wonderful. They deserve honest feedback, genuine standards, and the chance to discover what they're actually capable of when they're pushed to try. They deserve the possibility of excellence.

And we owe them the honesty to show them what it looks like.

FIFTEEN

STEWARDSHIP

The world is changed by the faithful, not the dramatic.
—Traditional proverb

My mother spent decades as a kindergarten teacher and Sunday school instructor. She filled rooms with stories, memories, observations, and a kind of warm, relentless narration of daily life. She never had a thought, my father used to kid her, that didn't come out of her mouth. She loved language – mostly spoken—the way some people love music—instinctively, unselfconsciously, completely.

She worked crossword puzzles daily. She enjoyed a nightly dose of *Wheel of Fortune*. She could talk to anyone—family, friends, strangers—and most days she did. Words were her medium, her joy, her way of being in the world.

Then aphasia came. Sudden and thorough.

At first, the words she'd used her whole life began drifting beyond her reach. Sentences frayed. Meanings loosened. The woman who had narrated everything eventually fell all but silent, not because she had nothing to say, but because the medium through which she'd always spoken had been taken from her.

Watching that happen taught me something no theory of language or philosophy ever could: when we lose our words, we lose more than vocabulary. We lose the structures that hold our memories, the tools that shape our relationships, and the bridges that connect our inner world to the outer one. Language is not decoration. It is identity. It is meaning. It is part of what makes us capable of connection, memory, and hope.

Her story is why I finally put my ideas about using words with precision into a book, why I pay attention to how words thin, and why I believe recovering depth in our language is not an academic exercise but a deeply human one. Words are not just sounds we make or symbols we write. They are how we become ourselves and how we make ourselves known to others. And when words fail—whether through illness or through the slow cultural erosion we've been tracing—something essential is lost.

The word that ties everything together—that names both the problem and the path forward—is *stewardship*.

Stewardship is an old concept that feels foreign to contemporary ears. We're not trained to think of ourselves as stewards. We're trained to think of ourselves as owners, consumers, users. We take what we want, use what we have, move on when it's exhausted. The idea that we might be responsible for maintaining things for others—for people we'll never meet, for generations not yet born—doesn't fit how we've learned to relate to the world.

But stewardship is what human thriving requires. Because we inherit more than we create. We're born into languages we didn't invent, traditions we didn't establish, institutions we didn't found, knowledge we didn't discover. All of this was given to us by people who came before, people who maintained and improved what they themselves inherited. And the question stewardship asks is: *What will we pass forward*?

This isn't primarily about environmentalism, though it includes that. It's about a comprehensive orientation toward everything we inherit and use. Are we leaving it better than we found it? Are we maintaining it for those who come after? Are we extracting value without returning anything? Are we consuming without replenishing?

The contemporary answer to these questions is mostly "No". We extract without maintaining. We consume without replenishing. We inherit without feeling obligated to pass forward. And we do this across every domain: natural resources, social institutions, intellectual traditions, cultural practices, and even language itself.

Let's look deeper at language. We inherit a rich, precise vocabulary built up over centuries—words with distinct meanings, subtle gradations, the accumulated wisdom of countless speakers refining meaning through use. What do we do with this inheritance? We flatten it. We make every word mean everything until words mean nothing. We treat language as infinitely malleable material for expressing whatever we feel in the moment, rather than as a shared resource that requires maintenance.

This is the opposite of stewardship. Stewardship would mean using language carefully, preserving distinctions, maintaining precision, passing forward a tool at least as useful as the one we inherited. But that requires viewing language as something we're responsible for, not just something we use. It requires thinking beyond our immediate expressive needs to the needs of people who will inherit our carelessness.

The same pattern appears everywhere. In institutions—we demand they serve our immediate needs without considering whether we're maintaining them for future needs. In communities—we extract what we want without contributing to their maintenance. In relationships—we take what we need without considering what we're giving back.

The failure of stewardship produces a particular kind of poverty: the poverty of inheritance. Each generation receives less than the previous one—not materially, necessarily, but in terms of maintained cultural goods. Thinner language. Weaker institutions. Shallower traditions. Depleted resources. And each generation, receiving less, passes forward less still.

This decline isn't inevitable. It's a choice. The choice to prioritize immediate use over long-term maintenance. The choice to view ourselves as consumers rather than stewards. The choice to ignore our responsibility to those who come after.

The recovery of stewardship requires recovering several things we've lost.

First, a longer time horizon. We have to think beyond our own lives, our own needs, our own satisfaction. We have to ask: What will exist after I'm gone? What will people inherit from my time here? Will they receive something maintained and improved, or something depleted and damaged?

This kind of thinking has become almost impossible in a culture optimized for immediate gratification. We're trained to think in quarterly returns, news cycles, election seasons. The idea of working for rewards we won't see, planting trees we won't sit under, building things we won't fully enjoy—it feels foolish. Impractical. A waste of limited time and energy.

But this short-term thinking is exactly what produces the poverty of inheritance. When no one thinks past their own lifetime, nothing gets maintained. Everything slowly degrades. And by the time the degradation becomes obvious, the work of rebuilding is exponentially harder than the work of maintaining would have been.

Second, a sense of gratitude for what we've inherited. When you recognize how much you've been given—how much was maintained for you by people you never knew—you feel the obligation to maintain it for others. Stewardship begins with acknowledging debt. Not guilt, debt. The recognition that you owe something to those who came before because they gave you something valuable.

Most people alive today benefit from institutions, knowledge, and freedoms that were built and defended by people who never lived to see the full fruit of their labor. The universities where we study, the hospitals where we're healed, the legal protections we take for granted, the accumulated scientific knowledge we inherit—all of this came at enormous cost to people who believed the future mattered enough to sacrifice for it.

When you lose sight of that debt, stewardship becomes impossible. Because without gratitude, maintenance feels like burden rather than obligation. It feels like you're being asked to sacrifice for strangers when you could be maximizing your own benefit. But with gratitude—with the recognition that you've received more than you earned—stewardship becomes the natural response. You maintain what you inherited because others maintained it for you.

Third, the humility to recognize that what you've inherited isn't yours to do with as you please. You're a temporary custodian, not an owner. This doesn't mean you can't change anything or improve anything. It means you approach change with caution, recognizing that traditions and institutions and practices often contain wisdom that isn't immediately apparent.

Contemporary culture has lost this caution entirely. We assume that old is obsolete, that tradition is oppression, that anything inherited must be examined, deconstructed, and probably discarded. And sometimes that's right. Not everything old deserves preservation. But the wholesale rejection of inheritance—the assumption that we're smarter than everyone who came before, that we can rebuild everything from scratch according to our own preferences—is arrogance, not wisdom.

Traditions survive because they work. Institutions persist because they serve functions that aren't immediately obvious. Practices endure because they've been tested over time. This doesn't make them perfect. It doesn't make them immune to criticism or reform. But it does mean they deserve respect—the kind of respect that tries to understand before it destroys, that asks why something exists before deciding it shouldn't.

Fourth, the willingness to do work that primarily benefits others. Stewardship isn't about improving your own life. It's about maintaining systems and resources and traditions that will outlast you. This requires a particular kind of generosity: working for rewards you won't receive, investing in futures you won't see, building things you won't fully enjoy.

This kind of work has always been rare because it runs against natural human inclination. We want to see the results of our labor. We want recognition for our contributions. We want to benefit from what we build. Stewardship asks us to accept that the best work we do might not benefit us at all—that its value might not become apparent until we're gone, that the people who benefit most might never know our names.

But this unnatural work is what makes human civilization possible. Because civilization is itself an act of stewardship—one generation maintaining and improving what it inherited so the next generation can do the same. When stewardship fails, civilization doesn't collapse immediately. It erodes. Slowly, imperceptibly at first, then faster. Until one day you realize that the things you thought would last forever have been lost.

Language is like this. You don't notice it degrading year by year. You notice it when you try to have a serious conversation and discover the words aren't there anymore. When you try to name something precise and find only vague approximations. When you try to build trust and realize the vocabulary for trustworthiness has been hollowed out.

Institutions are like this. They seem permanent until they're not. They seem self-sustaining until they collapse. And by the time you realize they needed maintenance, it's too late. The social trust required to build them has evaporated. The knowledge of how they worked has been lost. The people who knew how to maintain them are gone.

So the question stewardship asks each person is: What are you maintaining? What are you passing forward? What will exist because you were here that wouldn't exist otherwise?

These aren't comfortable questions. Because they reveal how much we take and how little we give back. How much we consume and how little we maintain. How focused we are on immediate satisfaction and how little we consider long-term consequence.

But they're necessary questions. Because without people willing to be stewards—without people willing to maintain what they inherited and pass it forward improved—nothing good lasts. Everything slowly degrades. And each generation inherits a thinner, poorer world than the one before.

The alternative requires a choice. The choice to be a steward rather than just a consumer. To maintain rather than just extract. To think beyond your own lifetime to lifetimes you'll never see. To work for rewards that will benefit others more than yourself.

This isn't heroic work. It's unglamorous, often invisible, rarely rewarded in ways that feel satisfying. But it's essential work. It's how good things persist. How valuable things get passed forward. How each generation gives the next something worth inheriting.

This book has been an attempt to name what's been lost and to suggest, carefully, how some of it might be recovered. Not through grand reform or institutional change, but through the small, unglamorous work of speaking more carefully, listening more generously, and refusing to let the words that matter most be thinned into meaninglessness.

Stewardship is the word that ties all of this together. It's the recognition that language is not ours to invent or discard—it's something we inherit, use for a time, and pass along. We are custodians of meaning. What we do with words during our brief turn with them shapes what the next generation will inherit.

If we let words become hollow, the next generation will inherit a hollowed-out vocabulary. If we use words carelessly, they'll learn carelessness. If we let precision collapse, they'll grow up unable to name what they feel or think with any clarity. But if we guard words, if we use them with intention, if we restore depth where it's been lost—then we give them tools that can actually build something.

Stewardship doesn't mean perfection. I've spoken carelessly more times than I can count. I've wounded people with words I wish I could take back. I've been shaped—often for better, sometimes for worse—by the same cultural forces I've been describing. Whatever insight exists in these pages comes not from mastery, but from paying attention. From noticing how words work on us, and how we work on them.

But stewardship does mean responsibility. It means recognizing that every time we speak, we're either strengthening language or weakening it. Every conversation either deepens trust or erodes it. Every sentence either clarifies meaning or clouds it. There's no neutral ground. Words are always doing something—building or thinning, connecting or isolating, revealing or obscuring.

The good news is that stewardship doesn't require eloquence. It doesn't require advanced education or literary talent. It just requires intention. The willingness to pause before speaking. The discipline to choose a truer word over an easier one. The humility to apologize when your words have caused harm. The patience to listen when someone needs to be heard.

These are small acts, but they accumulate. A workplace becomes more humane when people speak with respect. A family becomes stronger when words are used to build rather than tear down. A community becomes steadier when language retains enough precision to allow honest disagreement without collapsing into hostility.

The most important stewardship happens in the places no one else sees. In the tone a parent uses with a child when they're tired. In the way a spouse speaks during an argument. In the patience extended to someone who's struggling to articulate something difficult. In the refusal to participate in gossip. In the choice to tell the truth when a lie would be easier.

No one will applaud these choices. No one will write articles about them. But they matter. They shape the emotional and moral atmosphere in which everyone around you must live. And over time, they shape you. The person who practices generous speech becomes more generous. The person who practices patience becomes more patient. The person who refuses cruelty becomes less cruel.

Character and speech form each other. You don't wait until you're a good person to start speaking well. You become a good person, in part, by choosing words that align with the person you hope to become.

This is also why stewardship matters for children. They don't just need to be taught vocabulary—they need to be taught how language works, what it's for, why it matters. They need to see adults using words carefully, repairing mistakes, listening generously, speaking truthfully. They need to grow up in environments where speech has weight, where promises are kept, where apologies are real.

Children who grow up in such environments don't just learn words—they learn how to inhabit language in ways that build rather than destroy. They learn that speech is power, and that power can be used to protect or to harm. They learn that words reveal character, and that character is worth cultivating.

But children who grow up where words are cheap, where promises don't hold, where apologies are performative—they learn something else. They learn that language is a game, that sincerity is weakness, that nothing anyone says can really be trusted. And once that lesson is learned, it's hard to unlearn.

The recovery of language, then, is also the recovery of trust. Not naïve trust—trust that's been tested and proven reliable. The kind of trust that comes from dealing with people whose words match their actions, whose commitments hold, whose apologies are genuine.

That trust doesn't develop through speeches or policies. It develops through years of small fidelities. Through kept promises. Through words spoken with care. Through the accumulation of moments where someone chose honesty over convenience, clarity over performance, repair over defensiveness.

This is what we owe the next generation: not a perfect vocabulary, but a functional one. Not flawless speech, but honest speech. Not language used to manipulate or perform, but language used to reveal and connect.

We owe them words that still mean something. Words that can carry weight. Words that can build trust. Words that can name what's true, what's beautiful, what's good.

And we owe them the example of people who take language seriously—not because we're pedants or scolds, but because we know that words matter. That they shape reality. That they form relationships. That they reveal who we are and who we're becoming.

The world will not be changed by grand declarations or sweeping movements. It will be changed by the faithful—by people who quietly, steadily, without fanfare, refuse to let the things that matter become cheap.

Stewardship is that refusal, lived daily. It's the parent who corrects gently instead of harshly. It's the spouse who listens instead of lecturing. It's the colleague who speaks truthfully instead of politically. It's the friend who repairs instead of abandoning. It's the neighbor who engages instead of isolating. It's the citizen who speaks with clarity instead of slogans.

These are not heroic acts. They're ordinary ones. But ordinary acts, repeated faithfully over time, are what hold civilizations together. And when enough people practice them, the culture begins to shift—not dramatically, but perceptibly. The temperature cools. Trust grows. Conversations become possible that once felt dangerous.

Renewal doesn't announce itself with trumpets. It begins in the quiet spaces where someone chooses a better word, a clearer truth, a gentler tone.

My mother lost her ability to use words at the end. Her words and voice are gone. But the memory of her voice remains—warm, generous, full of life. And that memory reminds me every day that language is not permanent. It's fragile. It requires care. And we are its stewards.

What we inherit, we hold for a time. What we hold, we're responsible for. And what we're responsible for, we pass along—either strengthened or weakened by our use of it.

This book is my attempt to pass it along a little stronger than I found it. Not because I've mastered language, but because I love it. Because I've seen what happens when it fails. Because I believe the people who come after us deserve words that can still carry meaning, still build trust, still reveal truth.

The work of stewardship is never finished. Words will always be under pressure. Meaning will always be contested. Precision will always require vigilance. But the work is worth doing, because the alternative—a world where words mean nothing, where trust is impossible, where no one believes anything, anyone says—is unbearable.

We are not there yet. We can still recover what's been lost. We can still rebuild what's been weakened. We can still pass along a language capable of sustaining the next generation.

But only if we choose to. Only if we practice. Only if we refuse to settle for cheap speech, easy words, hollow promises. Only if we remember that language is not merely something we use. It is something we become. And what we become—patient or harsh, truthful or evasive, generous or cruel—will be written in the words we leave behind, long after we're gone. My parents and teachers taught me to love words before I understood their power. Now I understand. And that understanding is what I'm trying to pass along. Not perfectly. Not eloquently. But faithfully.

Because faithfulness, in the end, is what stewardship requires. And faithfulness is what the next generation will need, if they're going to have any words left worth speaking.

AFTERWORD — A LIFE AND LANGUAGE SHAPED BY BOOKS

This book did not begin as an argument or a project. It began with books—small ones, scribbled in by a toddler (me, circa 1966), and larger ones that opened wide worlds I had not yet lived long enough to imagine. It began with the *Childcraft: The How & Why Library* children's encyclopedias on my parents' shelf, and then my early graduation to the *World Book Encyclopedia*, which was the closest thing the 1970s had to a search engine for a boy who wanted to know everything at once.

It grew with *The Hobbit* and *The Lord of the Rings*, the paperbacks Santa brought in 1978, which still sit behind glass in my living room as if they're old friends who deserve a little protection. That same glass-enclosed bookcase also holds William Shakespeare and Arthur Conan Doyle, William Butler Yeats and J.K. Rowling, Margaret Mitchell and Rudyard Kipling. They are not trophies; they are waypoints—reminders of the voices that shaped me long before I ever thought to publish anything of my own.

I have always loved the look, the feel, and even the smell of books: the mustiness of used bookstores, the fresh ink aroma of a brand-new hardcover. More than once, someone has asked, half-jokingly, whether I would save the people or the books first if my house caught fire. I'm afraid they didn't care for my evasive answer, even if they weren't very surprised by it.

This book also began with teachers. High School English teachers Ms. Bond and Mr. Semore, especially, were among the first to show me that literature is not merely stories. It is a record of how human beings have thought, hoped, feared, and imagined across generations. It is the history of a culture thinking aloud. They showed me how the history of a people and the history of its language go hand in hand.

But the deeper truth is that this book began at home. When my children were young, they heard me say "Readers are leaders!" almost as often as they heard their own names. I never spoke baby talk to them because I wanted them to grow up inside the cadences of real language. Even today, when people meet my middle son—an intellectually disabled adult—they often initially misunderstand the depth of his disability because he speaks like the adults he heard at home. He limited only by the more extensive vocabulary that must be learned by reading.

I say all this because I want the reader to understand something essential: I did not write this book as someone who has *mastered* our language. I wrote it as someone who *loves* it. I have said careless things. More often than not, I have spoken too quickly. I have gone "low style" more times than I care to admit! Whatever wisdom is present in these pages did not come from perfection but from affection—affection for words, for the people my words touch, and for the fragile world that language helps us build.

If anything in these chapters feels weighty, it is not because I set out to lecture. It is because words have mattered to me for as long as I can remember, and I have learned—often the hard way—that how we speak to one another is one of the few things in life we can truly control.

This book is simply my attempt to honor the books, words, and language that first formed me, the teachers who guided me, and the family whose ears have heard every version of my voice.

And if these pages have led you to a word you needed, or returned you to a word you had forgotten, then this long affection has done its work.

READER'S GUIDE FOR GROUPS & INDIVIDUALS

A Note on This Guide

This guide is designed for a thirteen-week quarter. Some weeks pair two thematically related chapters whose arguments reinforce each other; other weeks give a single chapter the full session it deserves. The Further Study bibliography at the end serves as a reference throughout and becomes the launchpad for Week 13's synthesis conversation.

Week 1: The Thinning of Language

Introduction—The Philological Foundation

1. Before reading this book, had you considered that shifts in word meanings might reflect deeper cultural changes? Owen Barfield argued that "the history of a people lives inside their language." Choose one word from the book whose thinning surprised you most. How has the shift in that word's meaning affected conversations in your own life—at work, at home, in your community?

Week 2: Common Sense and Tolerance

Chapters 1–2—Two Failures of Social Perception

These two chapters form a natural pair: both examine our collective inability to acknowledge what is plainly visible.

2. Common Sense: Kipling's story of the white seal opens the chapter with an image of creatures returning to the same dangerous beach year after year out of habit. Before discussing what Gatlin does with that image: what drew you to it? Where in your own life—at work, at home, in your community—do you recognize that pattern? What makes it so difficult to say the obvious thing out loud?

3. Tolerance: Marcus Aurelius wrote: "Be tolerant with others and strict with yourself." Before you read this chapter, how would you have defined tolerance? How does that compare to the definition you'd give now? Can you think of a time when the word was used in a way that ended a conversation rather than opened one?

Week 3: Safety and Danger

Chapters 3—The Collapse of Risk Literacy

These chapters develop a single connected argument: protection without risk produces the opposite of what it intends.

4. Safety: The chapter opens with a specific example from a school that made a decision intended to protect children—and got an unexpected result. Did that example surprise you? Where else do you see the same dynamic: protection producing the opposite of what it intends? How do we distinguish reasonable precaution from something more harmful?

5. Danger: The chapter draws a sharp line between two words we often blur together. Before getting into the argument: in your own experience, what's the difference between danger and discomfort? Can you think of a time when you—or someone around you—treated one as the other? What happened?

Week 4: Courage and Heroism

Chapters 4–5—The Inflation of Virtue Language

Both words have undergone semantic inflation that strips them of their power to recognize genuine sacrifice and genuine risk.

6. Courage: C.S. Lewis called courage "the form of every virtue at the testing point"—not one virtue among others, but the condition that makes every other virtue possible when it becomes costly. Before reading this chapter, how would you have defined courage? Has that definition changed? Can you think of a moment when you or someone you know exercised courage in Lewis's sense—not dramatic, not announced, but costly?

7. Hero: The COVID-19 pandemic produced an enormous amount of "hero" language aimed at a very wide range of people. At the time, did any of that usage strike you as right? Any of it as wrong? What was the word doing in those moments—describing something, or performing something? What do we lose if the word can no longer make that distinction?

Week 5: Bigotry

Chapter 6—When Accusation Replaces Argument

8. This chapter takes on some of the most charged words in contemporary public life. Before getting into the argument: have you ever used one of these words—or had one used against you—and felt afterward that something had gone wrong in the conversation? Not that anyone was lying, but that the word itself had done something unexpected? What happened?

Week 6: Gratitude

Chapter 7—The Four Movements

9. Gatlin structures gratitude as something with distinct movements—more like a process than a feeling. Did that framing surprise you? How does it differ from how you typically think about gratitude—or how it's typically discussed in contemporary culture? Walk through a specific experience of your own using his framework. Where did it stall?

Week 7: Responsibility and Truth

Chapters 8-9—Accountability to Reality

Both chapters insist that reality does not accommodate our preferences—and that accepting this is liberating, not oppressive.

10. Responsibility: The chapter draws a sharp distinction between two words that are often used interchangeably. Before looking back at the text: in your own language, what's the difference between fault and responsibility? How does

Gatlin's distinction land—does it clarify something you already sensed, or does it push back against something you assumed?

11. Truth: The phrase "my truth" is now common enough that most people have heard it without questioning it. What does it mean? What does it assume? Before getting into Gatlin's argument—do you find the phrase useful, or does something about it make you uneasy? Where does it work, and where does it break down?

Week 8: Humility

Chapter 10—The Freedom to Say I Don't Know

12. C.S. Lewis wrote that "Humility is not thinking less of yourself; it's thinking of yourself less." Before getting into the chapter's argument: where in your life is it hardest to say "I don't know" or "I was wrong"? What would it cost you? What might you gain? How does the fear of appearing weak actually prevent growth?

Week 9: Reverence and Attention

Chapters 11–12—The Diminishment of Wonder

Both chapters diagnose the same underlying condition: a flattened capacity for encountering what is genuinely large.

13. Reverence: The chapter's subtitle asks a genuine question. Before getting into the argument: when did you last use the word "awesome" and actually mean it in the old sense—something that stopped you, that felt larger than your ability to describe it? What word did you reach for? Was it adequate? What does it tell us that we're reaching for the same words for very different experiences?

14. Attention: William James wrote: "We become what we pay attention to." Take that seriously for a moment before the discussion begins. Honestly assess your own attention patterns over the past week—not what you intend to pay attention to, but what you actually did. What are you becoming? Does that match who you want to be?

Week 10: The Language of Home

Chapter 13—Where We Become Who We Are

15. Think about the tone you use with those closest to you—spouse, children, parents. What patterns have formed without your conscious choice? How do your words at home differ from your words in public? What would repair look like in a relationship where careless words have accumulated? How do you model for children that mistakes can be acknowledged and relationships can survive conflict?

Week 11: Excellence

Chapter 14—The Cost of Abandoned Standards

16. Think of someone who held you to a standard—a teacher, a coach, a supervisor, a parent—in a way that felt demanding at the time but that you're grateful for now. What made it work? What distinguished that from criticism that didn't help? What does that experience tell you about what the word "excellence" actually requires?

Week 12: The Long View

Chapter 15—Stewardship Across Generations

17. Think about what you've inherited—in language, in traditions, in practices, in institutions—that you didn't build yourself. Who built it? What did it cost them? What are you now responsible for maintaining? What are you actively passing forward—and will the people who come after you have tools to build with, or burdens to manage?

Week 13: Synthesis

Bringing It All Together

Before this session, browse the Further Study section below and come prepared to discuss which resources you plan to explore and why. Then use the following questions to draw threads across the whole book.

A. Which of the fifteen words hit closest to home for you personally? Is there one whose recovery you've already begun—or one that feels most urgent for your community, your workplace, or your family?

B. Gatlin's project is fundamentally about recovery, not nostalgia. What's the difference? Is there a risk in wanting to recover older meanings? How do we do it without simply romanticizing the past?

C. Where do you go from here? Identify one concrete change you intend to make—in your own speech, in a conversation you've been avoiding, or in how you listen to language around you.

FURTHER STUDY

Essential Foundations in Philology

1. *Owen Barfield, Poetic Diction: A Study in Meaning* (1928) and *Speaker's Meaning* (1967) The philosophical foundation for Gatlin's entire project. Barfield demonstrates how semantic change reveals shifts in consciousness itself. Challenging but essential.

2. *C.S. Lewis, Studies in Words* (1960) Lewis traces the semantic history of words like nature, sad, wit, simple, and free, showing how their journeys reveal cultural transformations. Accessible and witty—perfect companion to this book.

3. *J.R.R. Tolkien, "On Fairy-Stories"* (essay, 1947) Tolkien's essay is fundamentally about language, sub-creation, and "recovery"—seeing things as they truly are by temporarily defamiliarizing them. Explains why stories and precise language matter for human flourishing.

Contemporary Cultural Criticism

1. *First Things* (magazine, firstthings.com) Monthly journal engaging religious and cultural questions with intellectual rigor. Particularly strong on how language shapes moral imagination and public discourse.

2. *The Hedgehog Review* (journal, iasc-culture.org) Published by the Institute for Advanced Studies in Culture at UVA. Explores therapeutic language, moral vocabularies, and how contemporary culture has thinned our capacity to name what matters.

3. *Alasdair MacIntyre, After Virtue* (1981) Philosophical examination of how modern moral language has become incoherent because we've lost the traditions that gave ethical terms their meaning. Dense but invaluable.

4. *Christian Wiman, He Held Radical Light* (2018) Poetry and prose exploring how modern spiritual language has become impoverished, and what recovery might look like. Beautiful writing about words that still carry weight.

Language, Thought, and Reality

1. *George Orwell, "Politics and the English Language"* (essay, 1946) Classic warning about how political corruption requires linguistic corruption. If you're only going to read one thing on this list besides Gatlin's book, read this.

2. *Neil Postman, Amusing Ourselves to Death* (1985) How media shapes consciousness and trivializes serious discourse. Complements Gatlin's concern about attention and depth.

3. *Wendell Berry, Standing by Words* (1983) Essays on language, agriculture, and culture. Berry's attention to how we speak about land and work parallels Gatlin's engineering precision about words.

The Inklings and Their Circle

1. *Diana Pavlac Glyer, The Company They Keep* (2007) How the Inklings influenced each other's work through conversation and friendship. Shows the collaborative nature of their linguistic and literary project.

2. *Malcolm Guite, Mariner: A Spiritual Biography of Samuel Taylor Coleridge* (2017) Coleridge's influence on Barfield and the Inklings' understanding of imagination, language, and meaning.

3. *The Marion E. Wade Center* (wheaton.edu/wadecenter) Archives and

resources related to the Inklings. Hosts conferences and maintains the world's foremost collection of their manuscripts, correspondence, and first editions.

Historical Perspective on Language and Culture

1. *Richard Weaver, The Ethics of Rhetoric* (1953) and *Ideas Have Consequences* (1948) How the words we choose reveal and shape our fundamental commitments about reality. Particularly relevant for understanding what Gatlin calls "the thinning."

2. *Josef Pieper, Leisure: The Basis of Culture* (1948) Philosophical meditation on contemplation, wonder, and the conditions necessary for meaningful thought and speech. Connects to Gatlin's chapter on attention.

Practical Application

1. *Vigen Guroian, Tending the Heart of Virtue* (1998) How stories—through precise, weighty language—form character. Particularly relevant for parents and educators concerned about passing forward strong vocabularies.

2. *Alan Jacobs, How to Think: A Survival Guide for a World at Odds* (2017) Accessible exploration of how to think clearly and speak carefully in polarized times. Practical wisdom for implementing Gatlin's vision.

3. *Marilyn McEntyre, Caring for Words in a Culture of Lies* (2009) Practical theology of language as stewardship. How Christians (and others) should approach public discourse with integrity.

On Memory, Aphasia, and the Loss of Words

1. *Jill Bolte Taylor, My Stroke of Insight* (2006) Neuroanatomist's account of her own stroke and aphasia. Illuminates what Gatlin experienced watching his mother lose language.

2. *John Hull, Touching the Rock: An Experience of Blindness* (1990) Not

about aphasia, but about the loss of another sense and how language must compensate. Profound meditation on what we lose when perception changes.

Online Resources and Journals

1. *The Davenant Institute* (davenantinstitute.org) Classical Protestant resources engaging language, culture, and retrieval of older intellectual traditions.

2. *The Calvinist International* (calvinistinternational.com) Theological and cultural commentary with attention to how Reformed tradition approaches language and public life.

3. *Plough Quarterly* (plough.com) Explores faith, culture, and community with attention to how we speak about what matters most.

4. *FORMA Journal* (formajournal.com) Published by CiRCE Institute. Focuses on classical education, including careful attention to language, logic, and the recovery of lost words.

For Engineering and Technical Readers

1. *Henry Petroski, To Engineer Is Human* (1985) On how precision in language and thought prevents catastrophic failure. Complements Gatlin's engineering background and his examples like the Challenger disaster.

2. *Samuel Florman, The Existential Pleasures of Engineering* (1976) On engineering as a humanistic discipline requiring precision in both language and mathematics. Bridges technical and philosophical concerns.

Memory, Family, and Loss

1. *Paul Kalanithi, When Breath Becomes Air* (2016) Neurosurgeon facing terminal cancer reflects on language, meaning, and mortality. Complements Gatlin's reflection on his mother's aphasia.

2. *Marilynne Robinson, Gilead* (2004) Novel structured as a father's letter to his young son, knowing he won't live to see him grow up. About what we pass forward in words when that's all we have left.

ABOUT THE AUTHOR

Jeff Gatlin is an engineer who has spent his career designing building systems across a wide range of industries and emphasizing—to junior engineers, students, and to the equipment operators on his teams—that technical excellence means nothing without the language to communicate it clearly and precisely.

He lives in Hernando, Mississippi with his wife Mary.